CORINNE MAIER - ANNE SIMON

FREUD

AN ILLUSTRATED BIOGRAPHY

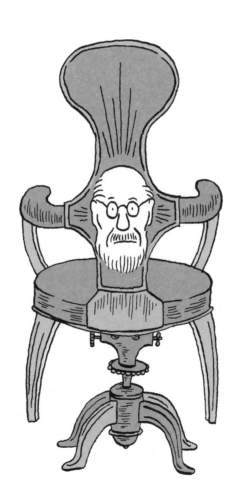

NOBROW

LONDON - NEW YORK

Corinne Maier is a noted psychoanalyst
and author of over 15 titles. "Hello Laziness"
and "No Kids" have both been translated into
the English language to critical acclaim.

Anne Simon was born in 1980 in France.
She studied in the Beaux-Arts in Angoulême,
and then in the École Nationale Supérieure des Arts
Décoratifs in Paris, one of the most prestigious art
schools in France. In 2004, she received the
"New Talent" prize at the Angoulême festival,
and she released her first comic book
"Persephone in the Underworld" in 2006.

FSC
www.fsc.org
MIX
Paper from
responsible sources
FSC® C118475

FREUD by Corinne Maier and Anne Simon.
All artwork and characters within are © 2012 DARGAUD.
This is a second English edition published in 2014 by Nobrow Ltd.
62 Great Eastern Street, London, EC2A 3QR.

Translated from French by J. Taboy. This translation is © 2013 Nobrow. Translation edited by A. Spiro.
This work has been done with the author's handwriting, digitalized into font by Lilian Mitsunaga.
Published by arrangement with DARGAUD. All rights reserved. No part of this publication may be reproduced
or transmitted in any form or by any means, electronic or mechanical, including photocopying, recording or
by any information and storage retrieval system, without prior written consent from the publisher.

Published in the US by Nobrow (US) inc.
Printed in Poland on FSC assured paper.

ISBN: 978-1-907704-73-4

Order from www.nobrow.net

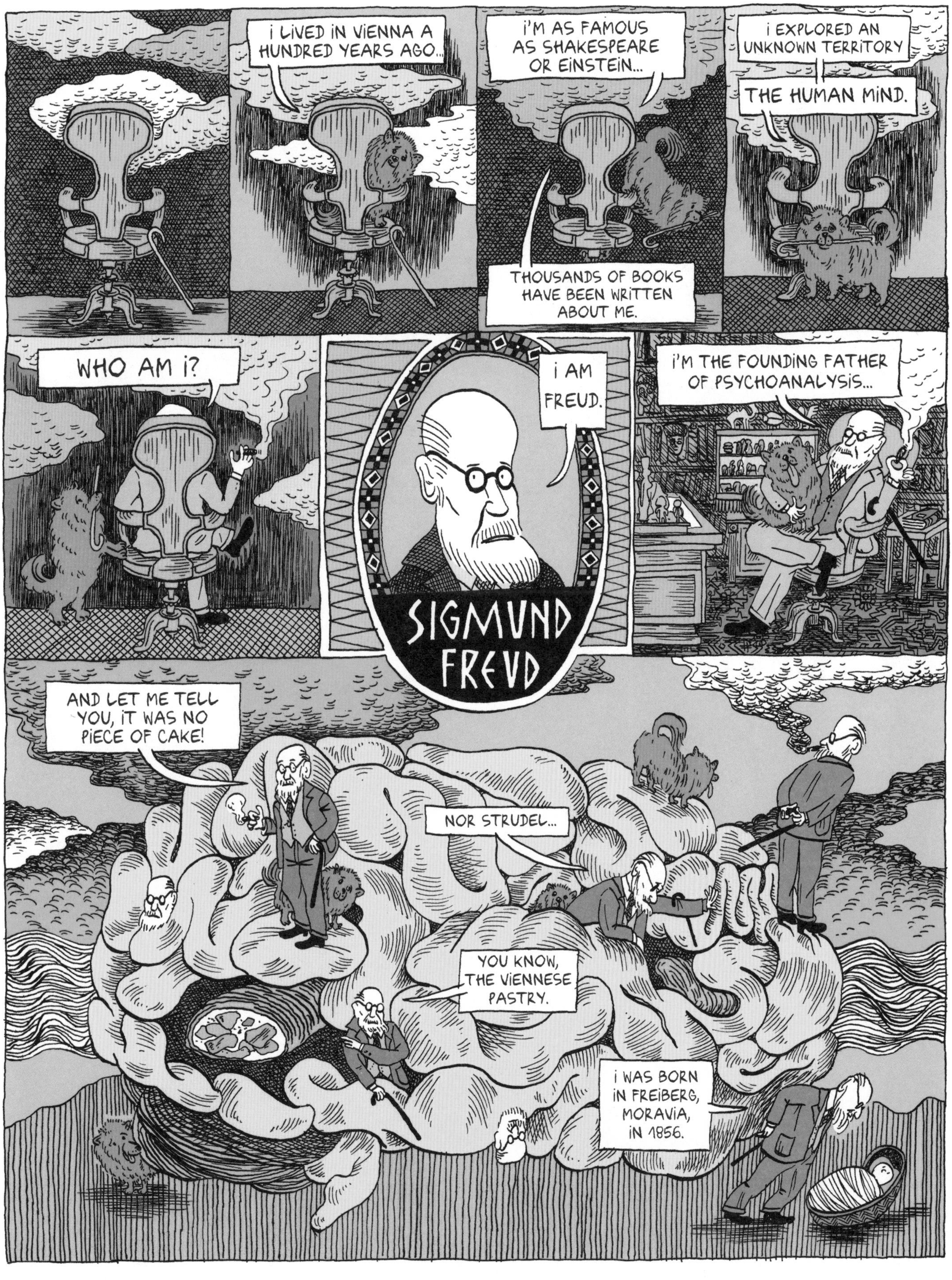
I LIVED IN VIENNA A HUNDRED YEARS AGO...
I'M AS FAMOUS AS SHAKESPEARE OR EINSTEIN...
THOUSANDS OF BOOKS HAVE BEEN WRITTEN ABOUT ME.
I EXPLORED AN UNKNOWN TERRITORY
THE HUMAN MIND.
WHO AM I?
I AM FREUD.
SIGMUND FREUD
I'M THE FOUNDING FATHER OF PSYCHOANALYSIS...
AND LET ME TELL YOU, IT WAS NO PIECE OF CAKE!
NOR STRUDEL...
YOU KNOW, THE VIENNESE PASTRY.
I WAS BORN IN FREIBERG, MORAVIA, IN 1856.

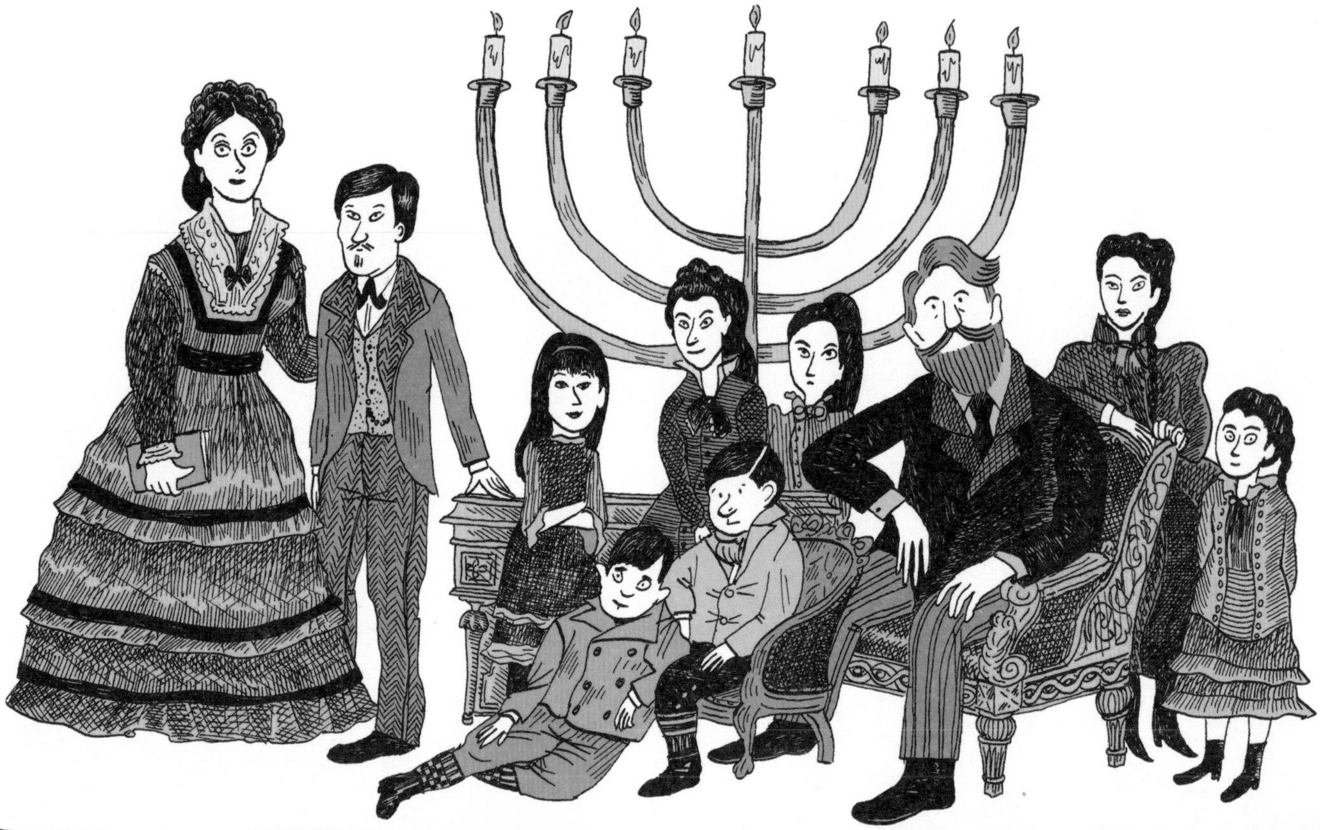

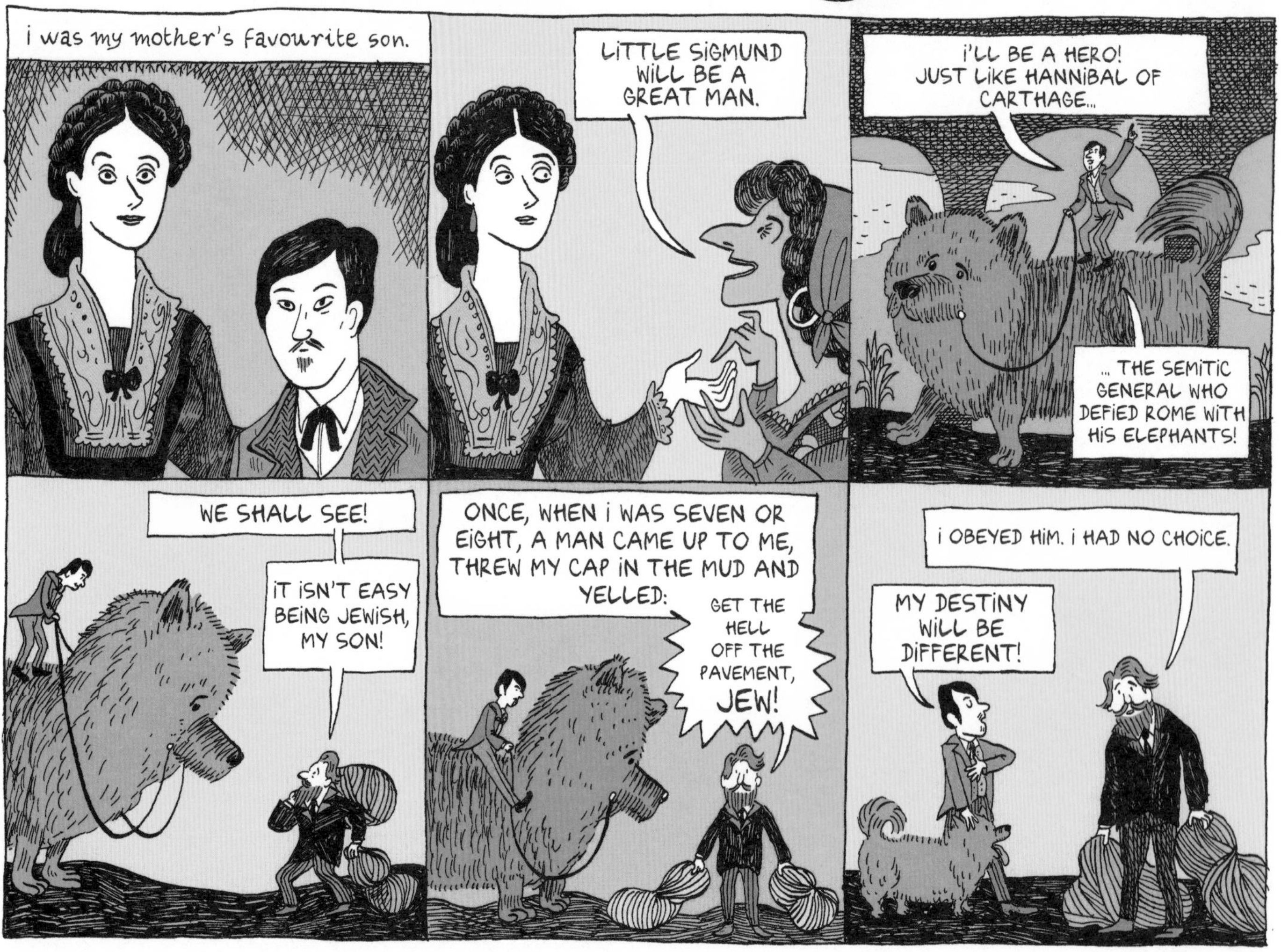
i was my mother's favourite son.
LITTLE SIGMUND WILL BE A GREAT MAN.
i'LL BE A HERO! JUST LIKE HANNIBAL OF CARTHAGE...
... THE SEMITIC GENERAL WHO DEFIED ROME WITH HIS ELEPHANTS!
WE SHALL SEE!
iT iSN'T EASY BEiNG JEWiSH, MY SON!
ONCE, WHEN i WAS SEVEN OR EiGHT, A MAN CAME UP TO ME, THREW MY CAP iN THE MUD AND YELLED:
GET THE HELL OFF THE PAVEMENT, JEW!
i OBEYED HiM. i HAD NO CHOiCE.
MY DESTiNY WiLL BE DiFFERENT!

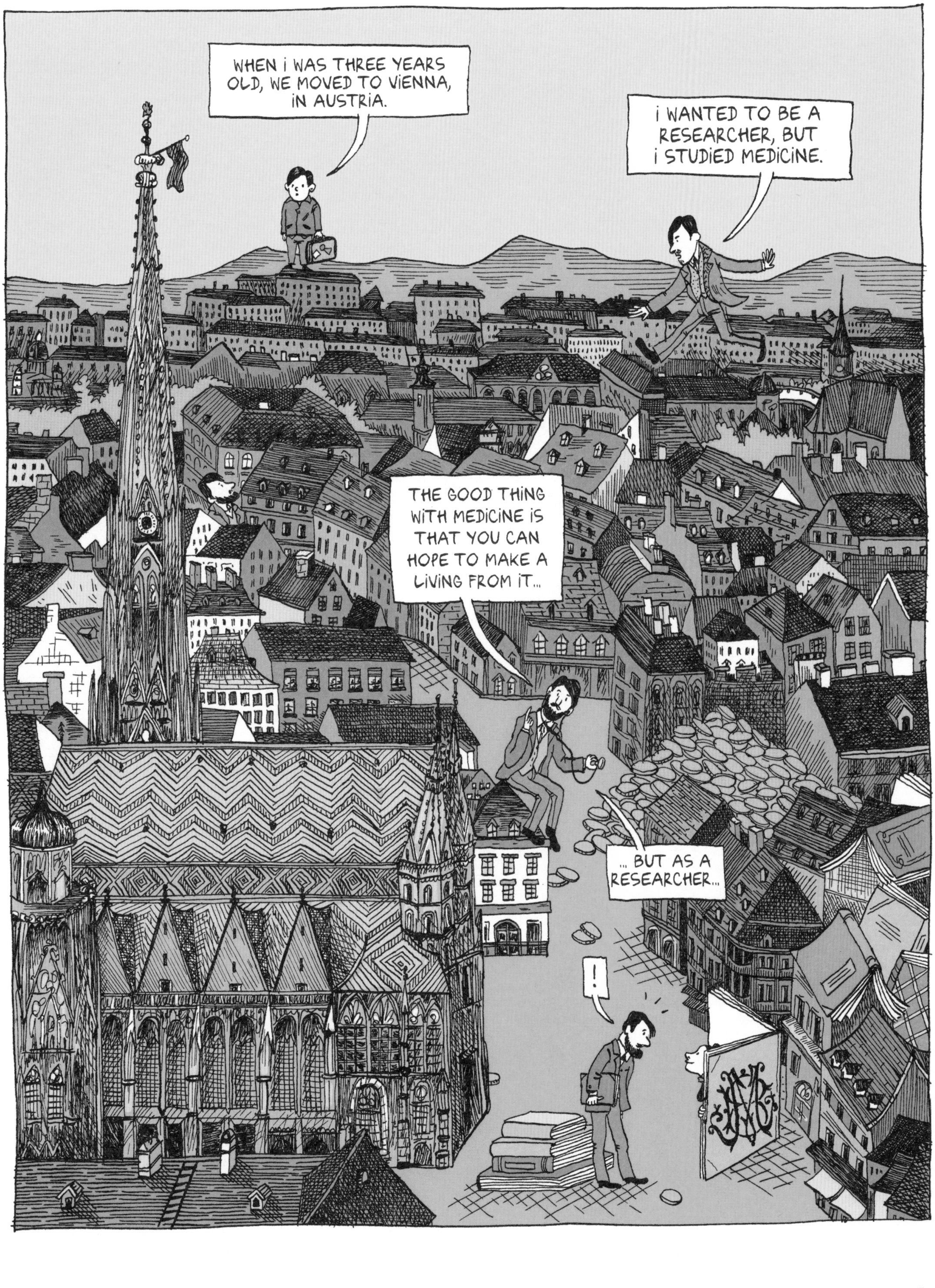
WHEN I WAS THREE YEARS OLD, WE MOVED TO VIENNA, IN AUSTRIA.
I WANTED TO BE A RESEARCHER, BUT I STUDIED MEDICINE.
THE GOOD THING WITH MEDICINE IS THAT YOU CAN HOPE TO MAKE A LIVING FROM IT...
... BUT AS A RESEARCHER...
!

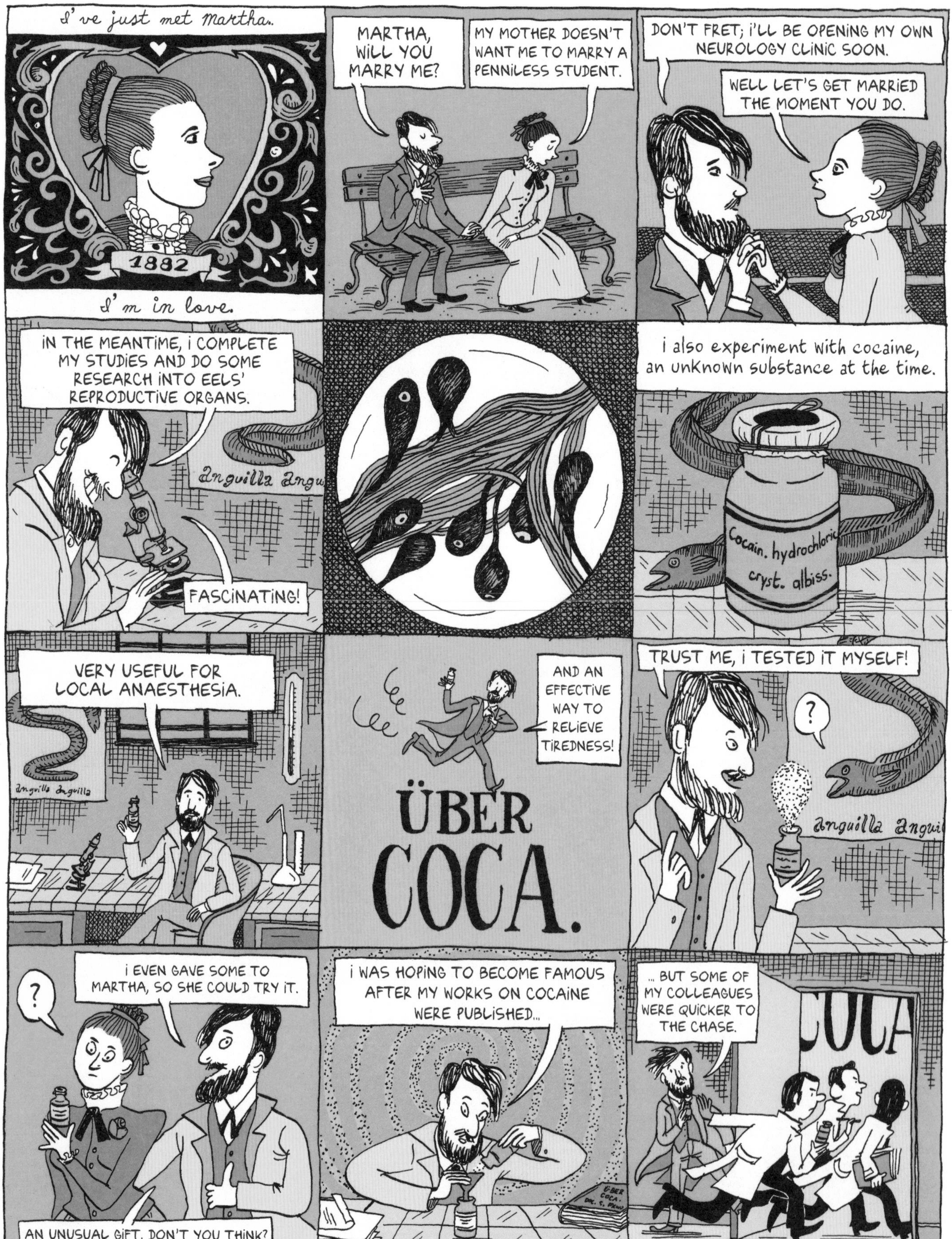

I've just met Martha.
1882
I'm in love.
MARTHA, WILL YOU MARRY ME?
MY MOTHER DOESN'T WANT ME TO MARRY A PENNILESS STUDENT.
DON'T FRET; I'LL BE OPENING MY OWN NEUROLOGY CLINIC SOON.
WELL LET'S GET MARRIED THE MOMENT YOU DO.
IN THE MEANTIME, I COMPLETE MY STUDIES AND DO SOME RESEARCH INTO EELS' REPRODUCTIVE ORGANS.
Anguilla angu
FASCINATING!
i also experiment with cocaine, an unknown substance at the time.
Cocain. hydrochloric cryst. albiss.
VERY USEFUL FOR LOCAL ANAESTHESIA.
Anguilla Anguilla
AND AN EFFECTIVE WAY TO RELIEVE TIREDNESS!
ÜBER COCA.
TRUST ME, I TESTED IT MYSELF!
?
Anguilla angu
?
I EVEN GAVE SOME TO MARTHA, SO SHE COULD TRY IT.
AN UNUSUAL GIFT, DON'T YOU THINK?
I WAS HOPING TO BECOME FAMOUS AFTER MY WORKS ON COCAINE WERE PUBLISHED...
... BUT SOME OF MY COLLEAGUES WERE QUICKER TO THE CHASE.
COCA

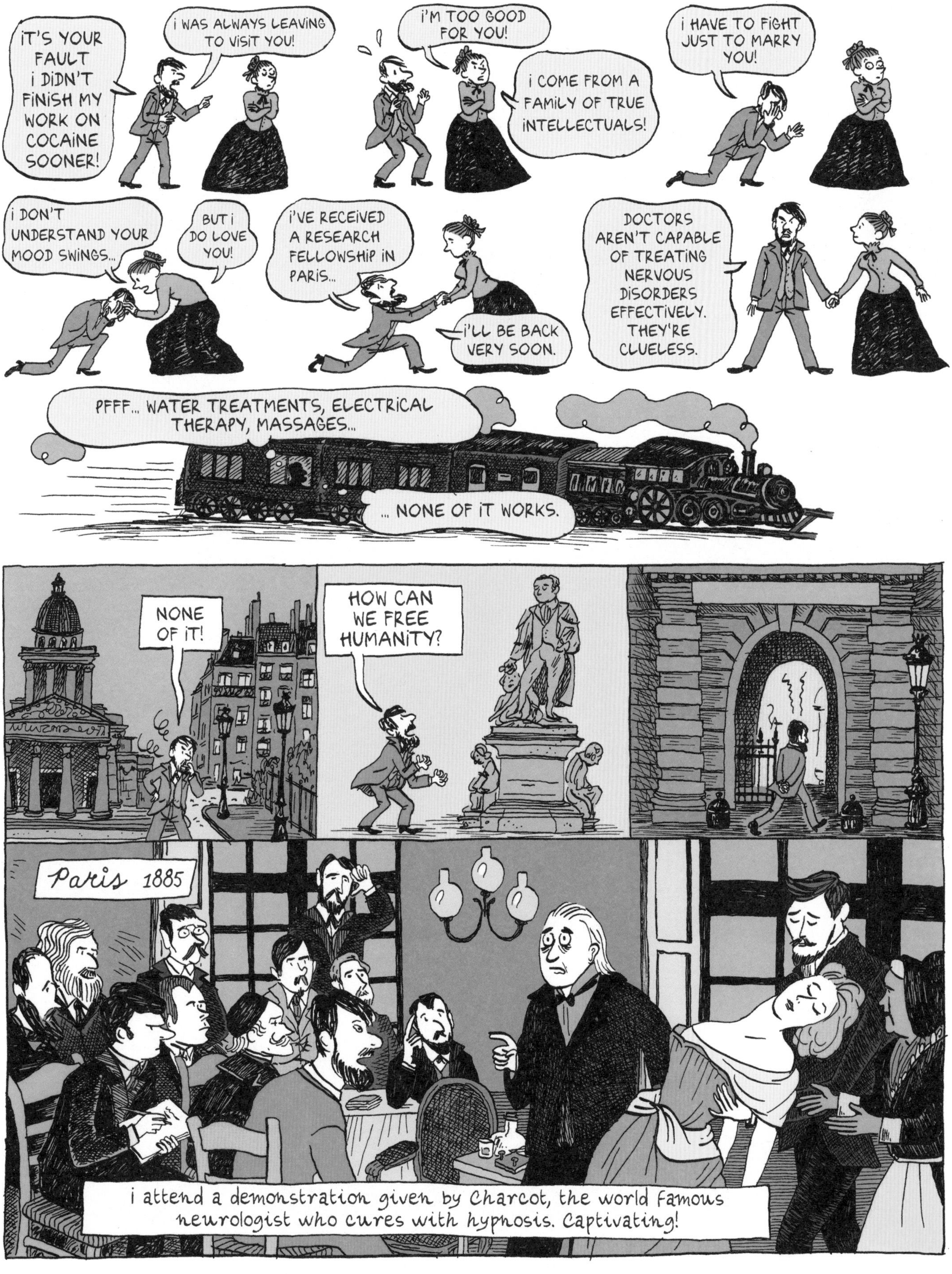

IT'S YOUR FAULT I DIDN'T FINISH MY WORK ON COCAINE SOONER!
I WAS ALWAYS LEAVING TO VISIT YOU!
I'M TOO GOOD FOR YOU!
I COME FROM A FAMILY OF TRUE INTELLECTUALS!
I HAVE TO FIGHT JUST TO MARRY YOU!
I DON'T UNDERSTAND YOUR MOOD SWINGS...
BUT I DO LOVE YOU!
I'VE RECEIVED A RESEARCH FELLOWSHIP IN PARIS...
I'LL BE BACK VERY SOON.
DOCTORS AREN'T CAPABLE OF TREATING NERVOUS DISORDERS EFFECTIVELY. THEY'RE CLUELESS.
PFFF... WATER TREATMENTS, ELECTRICAL THERAPY, MASSAGES...
... NONE OF IT WORKS.
NONE OF IT!
HOW CAN WE FREE HUMANITY?
Paris 1885
I attend a demonstration given by Charcot, the world famous neurologist who cures with hypnosis. Captivating!

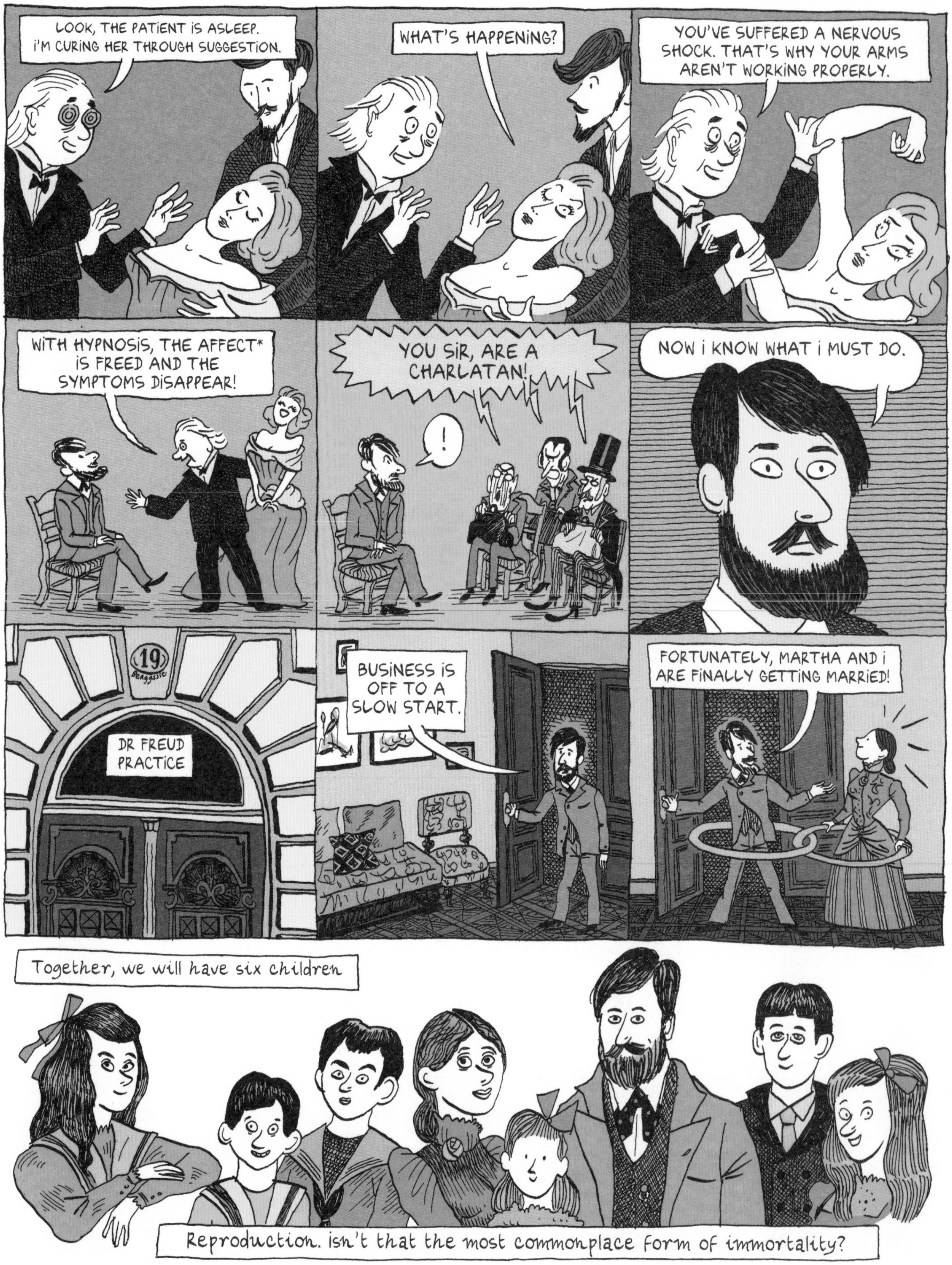
LOOK, THE PATIENT IS ASLEEP. I'M CURING HER THROUGH SUGGESTION.
WHAT'S HAPPENING?
YOU'VE SUFFERED A NERVOUS SHOCK. THAT'S WHY YOUR ARMS AREN'T WORKING PROPERLY.
WITH HYPNOSIS, THE AFFECT* IS FREED AND THE SYMPTOMS DISAPPEAR!
YOU SIR, ARE A CHARLATAN!
!
NOW I KNOW WHAT I MUST DO.
19
DR FREUD PRACTICE
BUSINESS IS OFF TO A SLOW START.
FORTUNATELY, MARTHA AND I ARE FINALLY GETTING MARRIED!
Together, we will have six children
Reproduction. isn't that the most commonplace form of immortality?

*AFFECT: Affect is a psychological term referring to emotions and feelings.

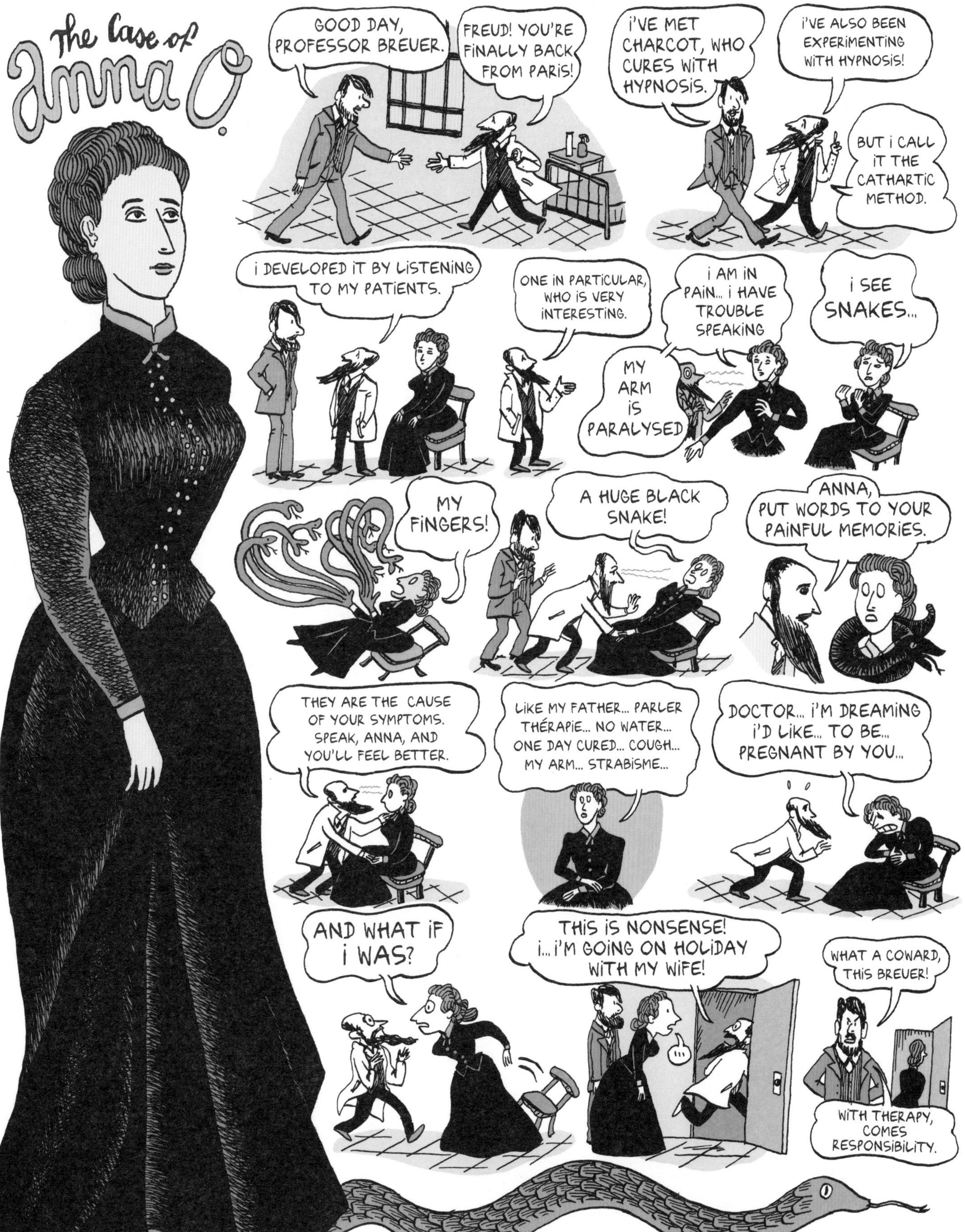
The Case of Anna O.
GOOD DAY, PROFESSOR BREUER.
FREUD! YOU'RE FINALLY BACK FROM PARIS!
I'VE MET CHARCOT, WHO CURES WITH HYPNOSIS.
I'VE ALSO BEEN EXPERIMENTING WITH HYPNOSIS!
BUT I CALL IT THE CATHARTIC METHOD.
I DEVELOPED IT BY LISTENING TO MY PATIENTS.
ONE IN PARTICULAR, WHO IS VERY INTERESTING.
I AM IN PAIN... I HAVE TROUBLE SPEAKING
MY ARM IS PARALYSED
I SEE SNAKES...
MY FINGERS!
A HUGE BLACK SNAKE!
ANNA, PUT WORDS TO YOUR PAINFUL MEMORIES.
THEY ARE THE CAUSE OF YOUR SYMPTOMS. SPEAK, ANNA, AND YOU'LL FEEL BETTER.
LIKE MY FATHER... PARLER THÉRAPIE... NO WATER... ONE DAY CURED... COUGH... MY ARM... STRABISME...
DOCTOR... I'M DREAMING I'D LIKE... TO BE... PREGNANT BY YOU...
AND WHAT IF I WAS?
THIS IS NONSENSE! I... I'M GOING ON HOLIDAY WITH MY WIFE!
WHAT A COWARD, THIS BREUER!
WITH THERAPY, COMES RESPONSIBILITY.

FREUD'S METHOD

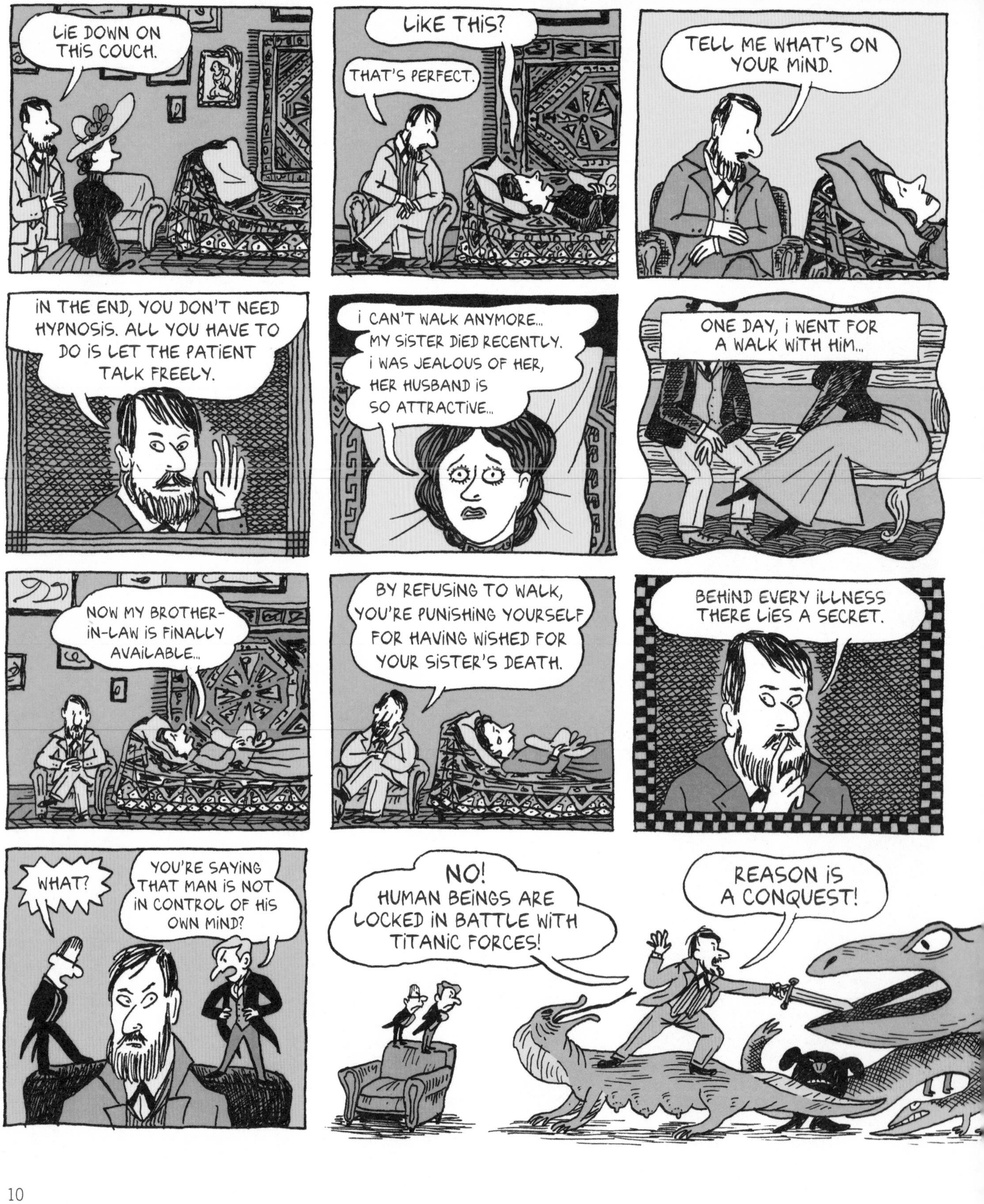
LIE DOWN ON THIS COUCH.
LIKE THIS?
THAT'S PERFECT.
TELL ME WHAT'S ON YOUR MIND.
IN THE END, YOU DON'T NEED HYPNOSIS. ALL YOU HAVE TO DO IS LET THE PATIENT TALK FREELY.
I CAN'T WALK ANYMORE... MY SISTER DIED RECENTLY. I WAS JEALOUS OF HER, HER HUSBAND IS SO ATTRACTIVE...
ONE DAY, I WENT FOR A WALK WITH HIM...
NOW MY BROTHER-IN-LAW IS FINALLY AVAILABLE...
BY REFUSING TO WALK, YOU'RE PUNISHING YOURSELF FOR HAVING WISHED FOR YOUR SISTER'S DEATH.
BEHIND EVERY ILLNESS THERE LIES A SECRET.
WHAT?
YOU'RE SAYING THAT MAN IS NOT IN CONTROL OF HIS OWN MIND?
NO! HUMAN BEINGS ARE LOCKED IN BATTLE WITH TITANIC FORCES!
REASON IS A CONQUEST!

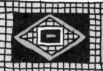

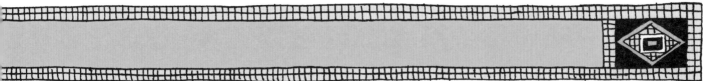

YOU HAVE TO LISTEN CAREFULLY.

THE UNCONSCIOUS MIND IS CRAFTY.

IT HIDES BEHIND A MASK.

LET ME TELL YOU A JEWISH STORY I REALLY LIKE.

A man lends a cauldron to his neighbour.

The neighbour gives it back.

THERE IS A HOLE IN MY CAULDRON!

I NEVER BORROWED YOUR CAULDRON!

BESIDES, THERE WAS A HOLE IN IT WHEN YOU GAVE IT TO ME.

I GAVE IT BACK IN GOOD CONDITION!

THESE DENIALS HIDE HIS UNCONSCIOUS DESIRE: HE'S JEALOUS OF HIS NEIGHBOUR.

IF YOU KNOW HOW TO LISTEN, ALL CAN BE REVEALED.

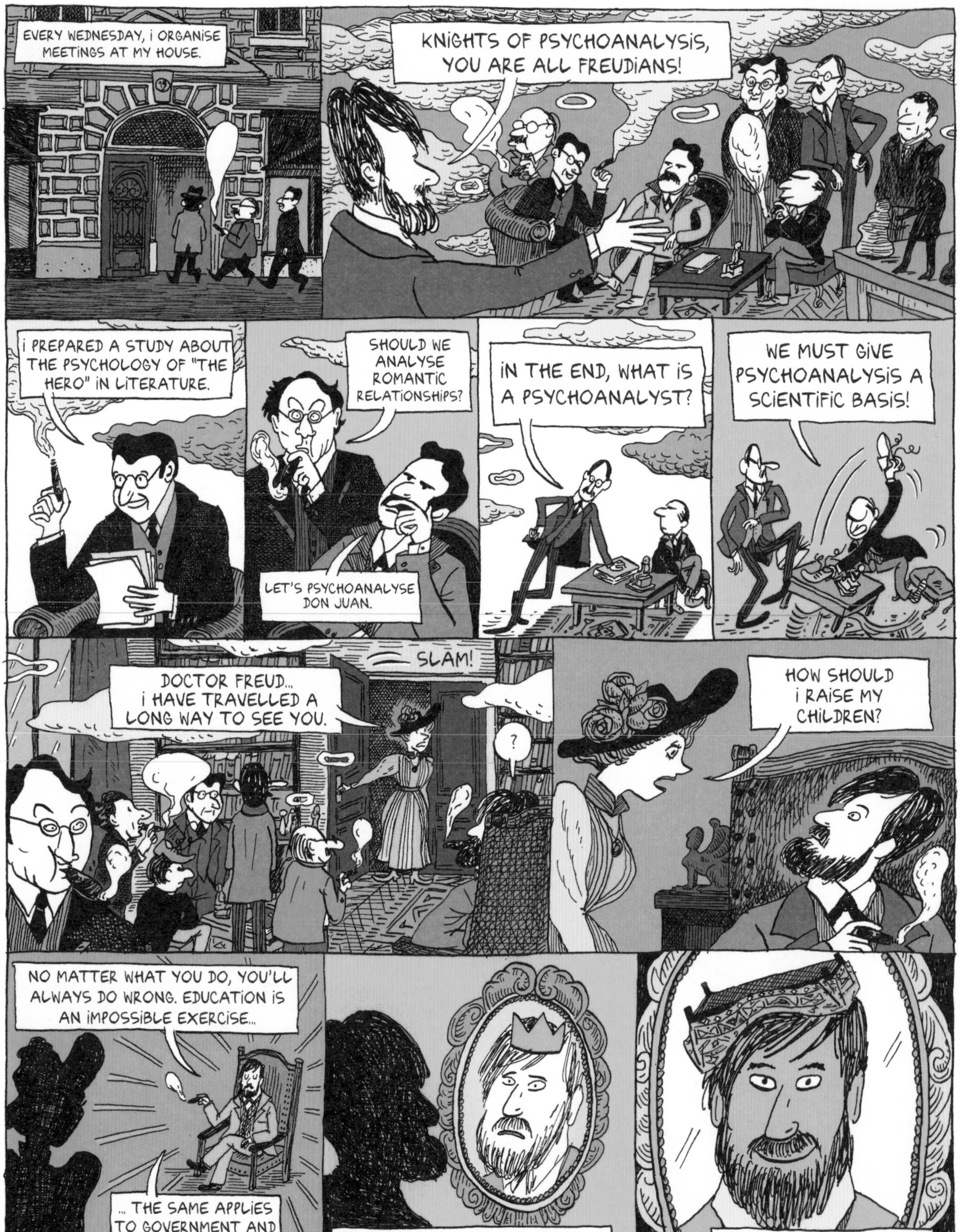
EVERY WEDNESDAY, I ORGANISE MEETINGS AT MY HOUSE.
KNIGHTS OF PSYCHOANALYSIS, YOU ARE ALL FREUDIANS!
I PREPARED A STUDY ABOUT THE PSYCHOLOGY OF "THE HERO" IN LITERATURE.
SHOULD WE ANALYSE ROMANTIC RELATIONSHIPS?
LET'S PSYCHOANALYSE DON JUAN.
IN THE END, WHAT IS A PSYCHOANALYST?
WE MUST GIVE PSYCHOANALYSIS A SCIENTIFIC BASIS!
DOCTOR FREUD... I HAVE TRAVELLED A LONG WAY TO SEE YOU.
SLAM!
?
HOW SHOULD I RAISE MY CHILDREN?
NO MATTER WHAT YOU DO, YOU'LL ALWAYS DO WRONG. EDUCATION IS AN IMPOSSIBLE EXERCISE...
... THE SAME APPLIES TO GOVERNMENT AND PSYCHOANALYSIS.
YES, I KNOW, I'M RIDICULOUS.
MY KINGDOM FOR A COUCH.

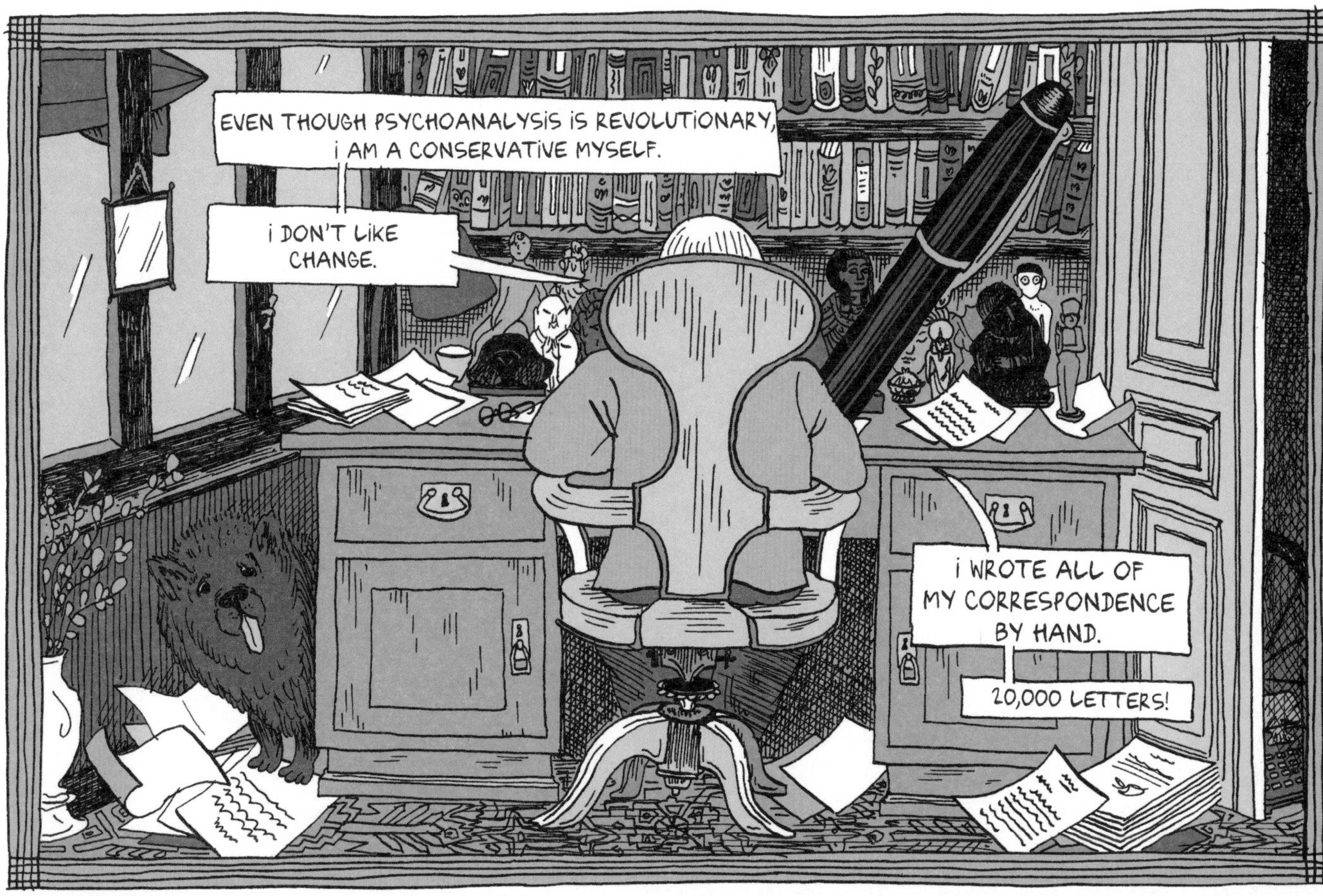
EVEN THOUGH PSYCHOANALYSIS IS REVOLUTIONARY, I AM A CONSERVATIVE MYSELF.
I DON'T LIKE CHANGE.
I WROTE ALL OF MY CORRESPONDENCE BY HAND.
20,000 LETTERS!

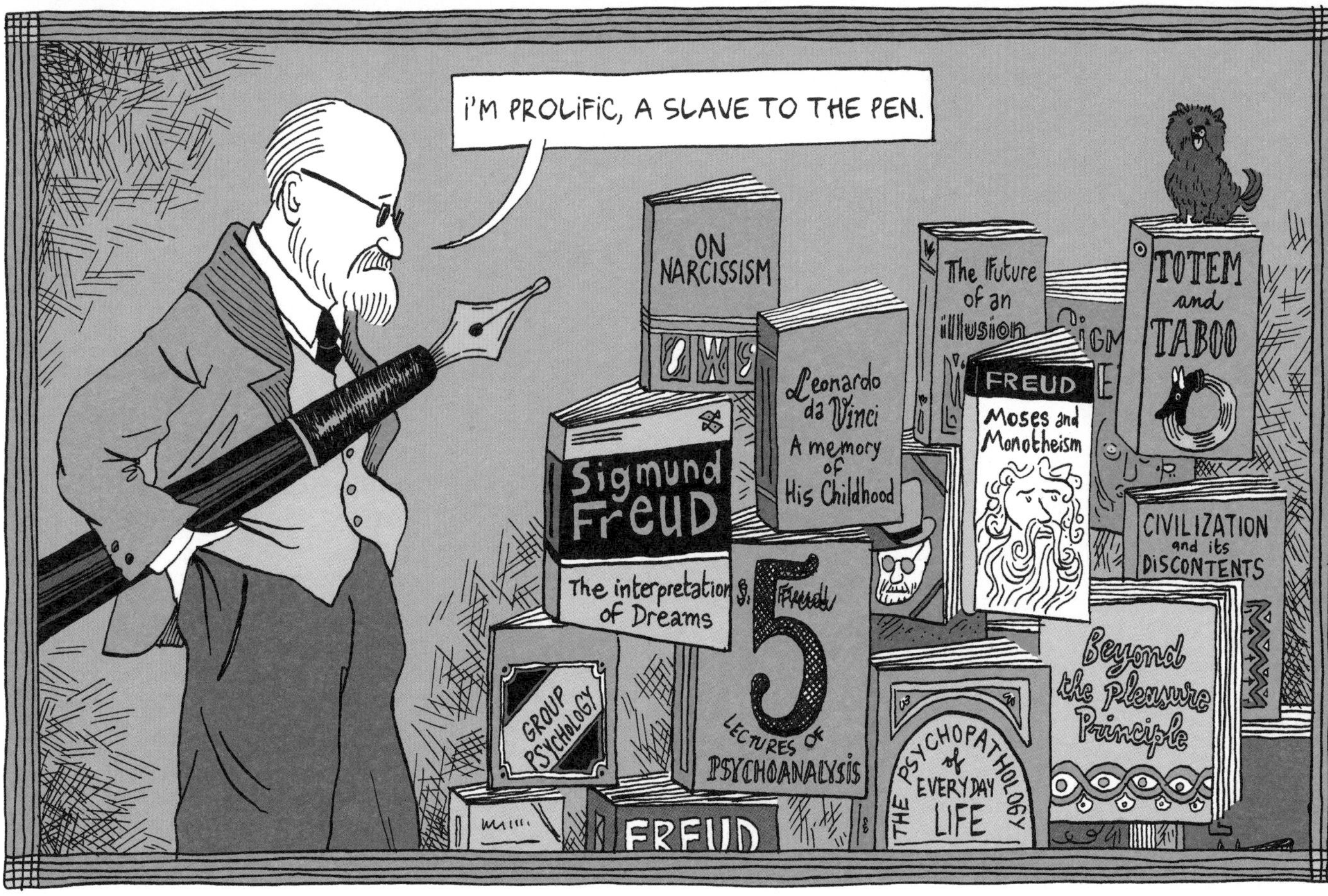
I'M PROLIFIC, A SLAVE TO THE PEN.
ON NARCISSISM
The Future of an illusion
TOTEM and TABOO
Leonardo da Vinci A memory of His Childhood
FREUD Moses and Monotheism
Sigmund Freud The interpretation of Dreams
CIVILIZATION and its DISCONTENTS
5 LECTURES OF PSYCHOANALYSIS
Beyond the Pleasure Principle
GROUP PSYCHOLOGY
THE PSYCHOPATHOLOGY of EVERYDAY LIFE
FREUD

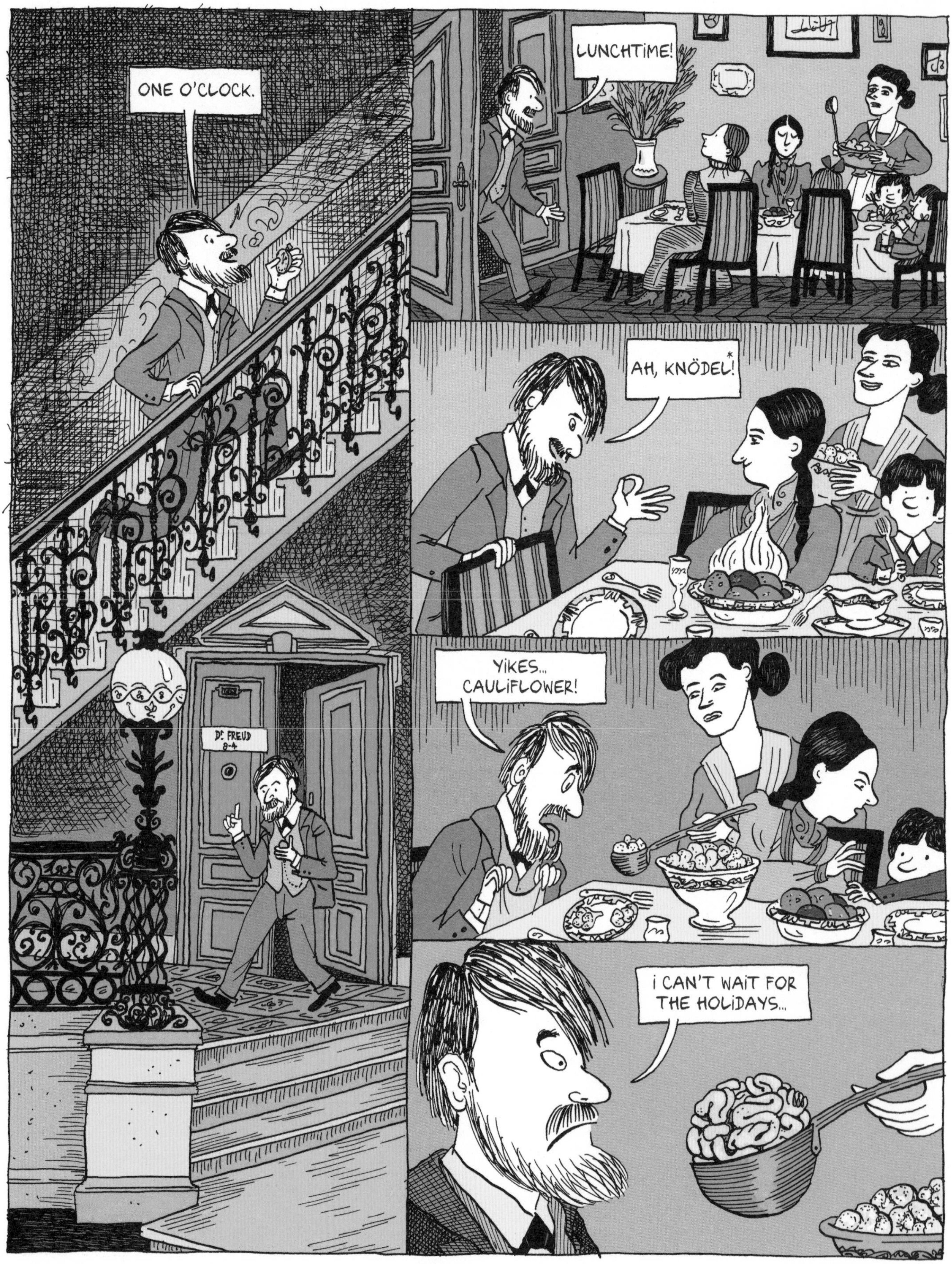
ONE O'CLOCK.
Dr. FREUD 8-4
LUNCHTIME!
AH, KNÖDEL!*
YIKES... CAULIFLOWER!
I CAN'T WAIT FOR THE HOLIDAYS...

* KNÖDEL: bread or potato dumplings, Austrian delicacy.

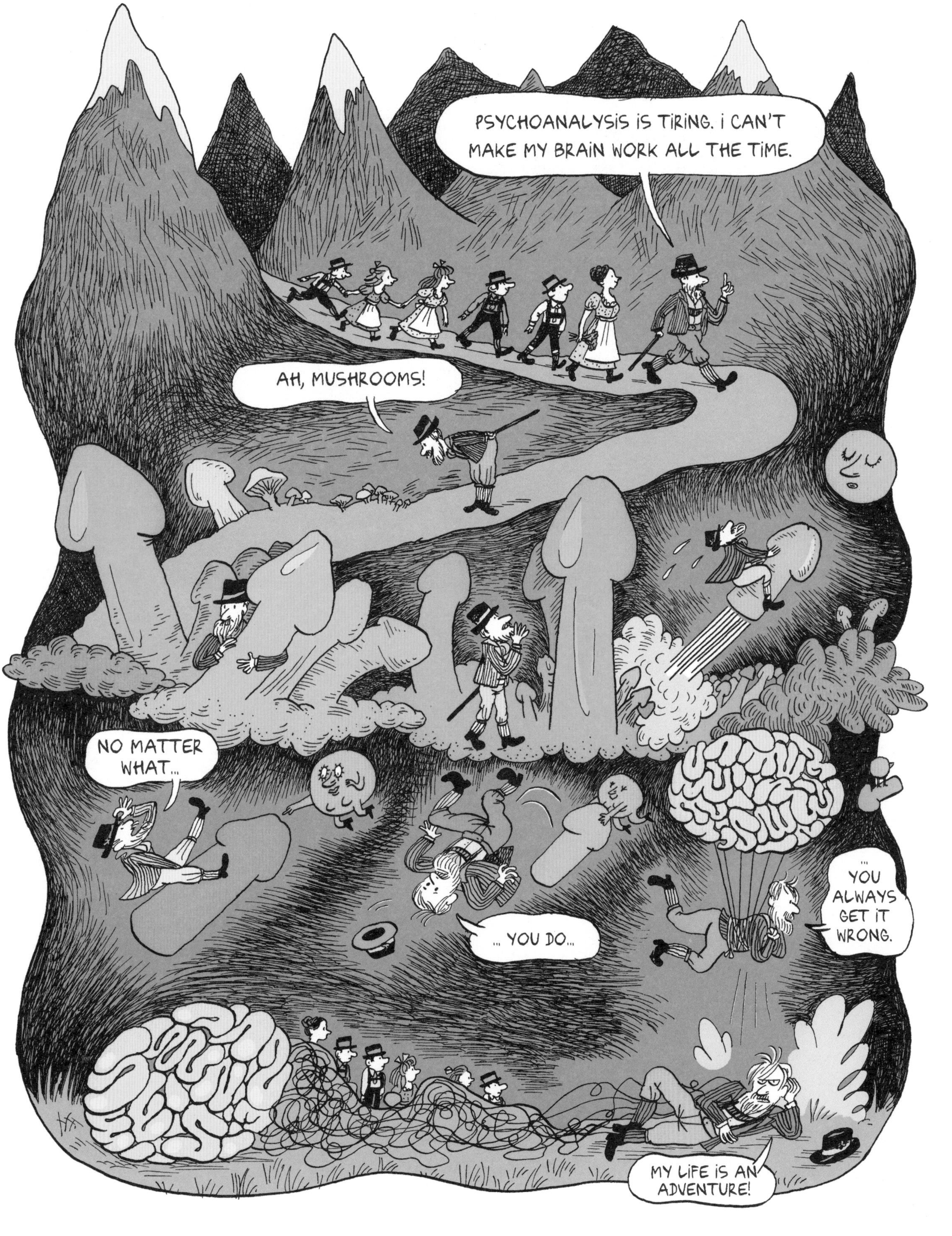
PSYCHOANALYSIS IS TIRING. I CAN'T MAKE MY BRAIN WORK ALL THE TIME.
AH, MUSHROOMS!
NO MATTER WHAT...
... YOU DO...
... YOU ALWAYS GET IT WRONG.
MY LIFE IS AN ADVENTURE!

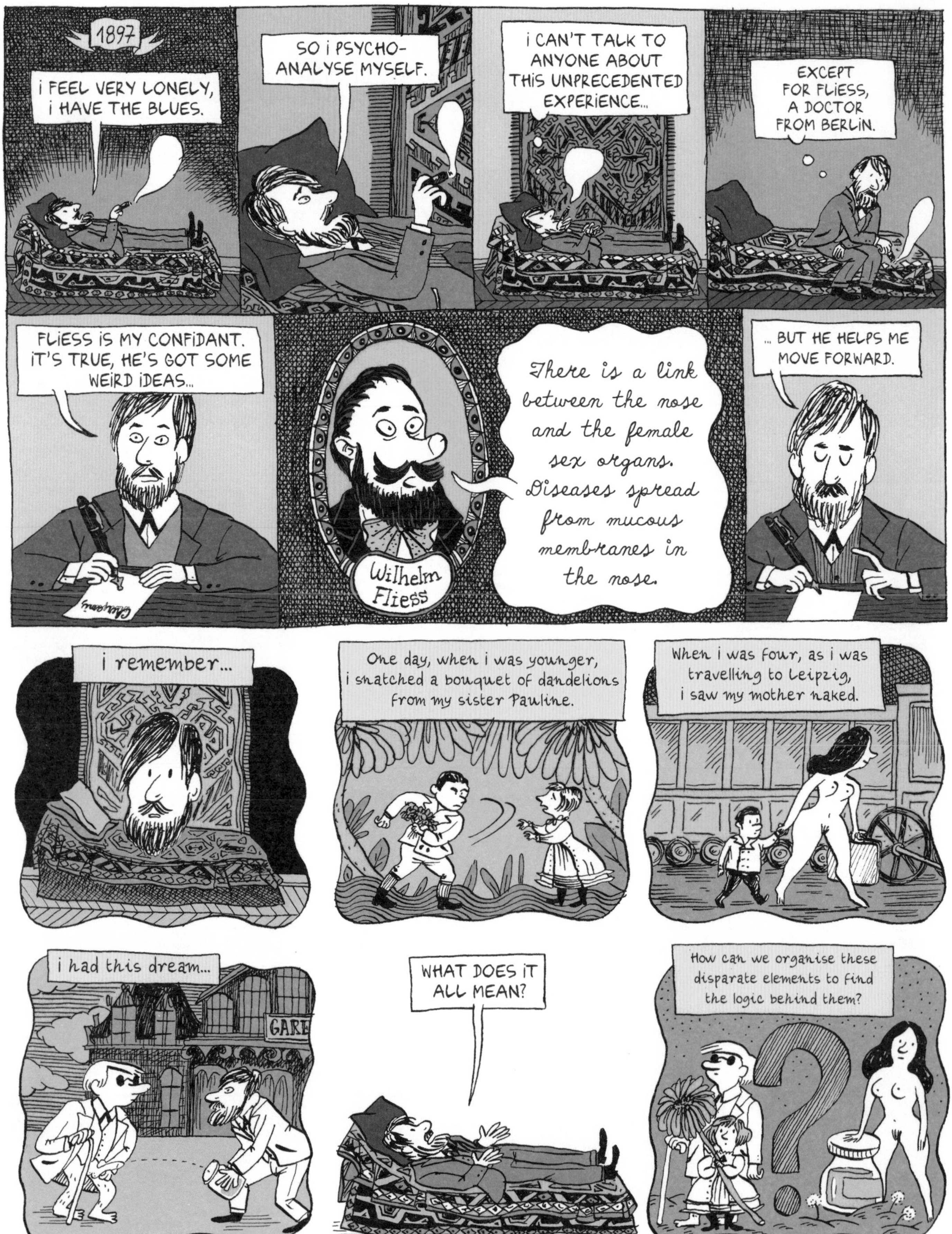

1897
i FEEL VERY LONELY, i HAVE THE BLUES.
SO i PSYCHO-ANALYSE MYSELF.
i CAN'T TALK TO ANYONE ABOUT THIS UNPRECEDENTED EXPERIENCE...
EXCEPT FOR FLiESS, A DOCTOR FROM BERLiN.
FLiESS iS MY CONFiDANT. iT'S TRUE, HE'S GOT SOME WEiRD iDEAS...
Wilhelm Fliess
There is a link between the nose and the female sex organs. Diseases spread from mucous membranes in the nose.
... BUT HE HELPS ME MOVE FORWARD.
i remember...
One day, when i was younger, i snatched a bouquet of dandelions from my sister Pauline.
When i was four, as i was travelling to Leipzig, i saw my mother naked.
i had this dream...
GARE
WHAT DOES iT ALL MEAN?
How can we organise these disparate elements to find the logic behind them?

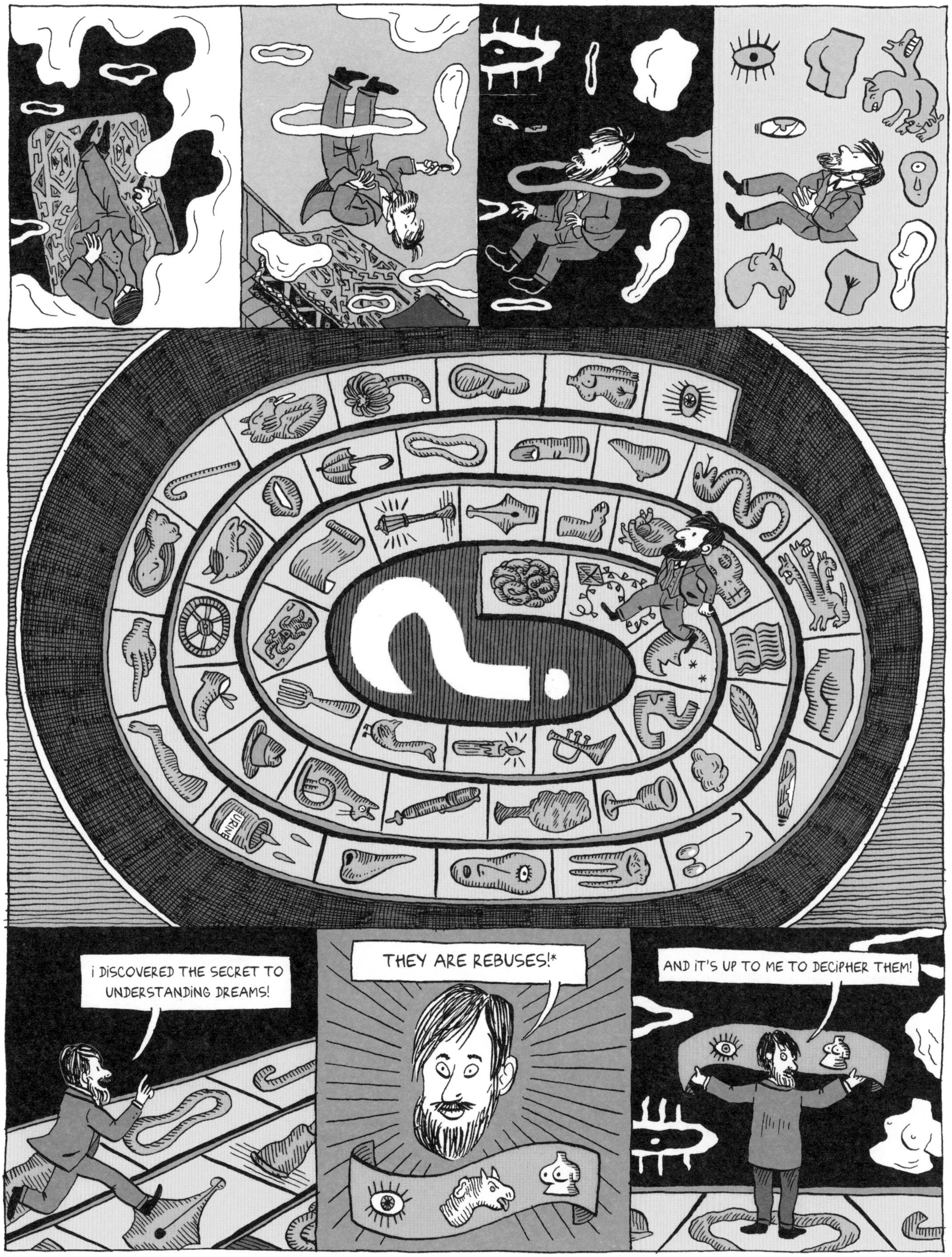
I DISCOVERED THE SECRET TO UNDERSTANDING DREAMS!
THEY ARE REBUSES!*
AND IT'S UP TO ME TO DECIPHER THEM!

*REBUS: A puzzle that uses a combination of pictures and numbers to make words.

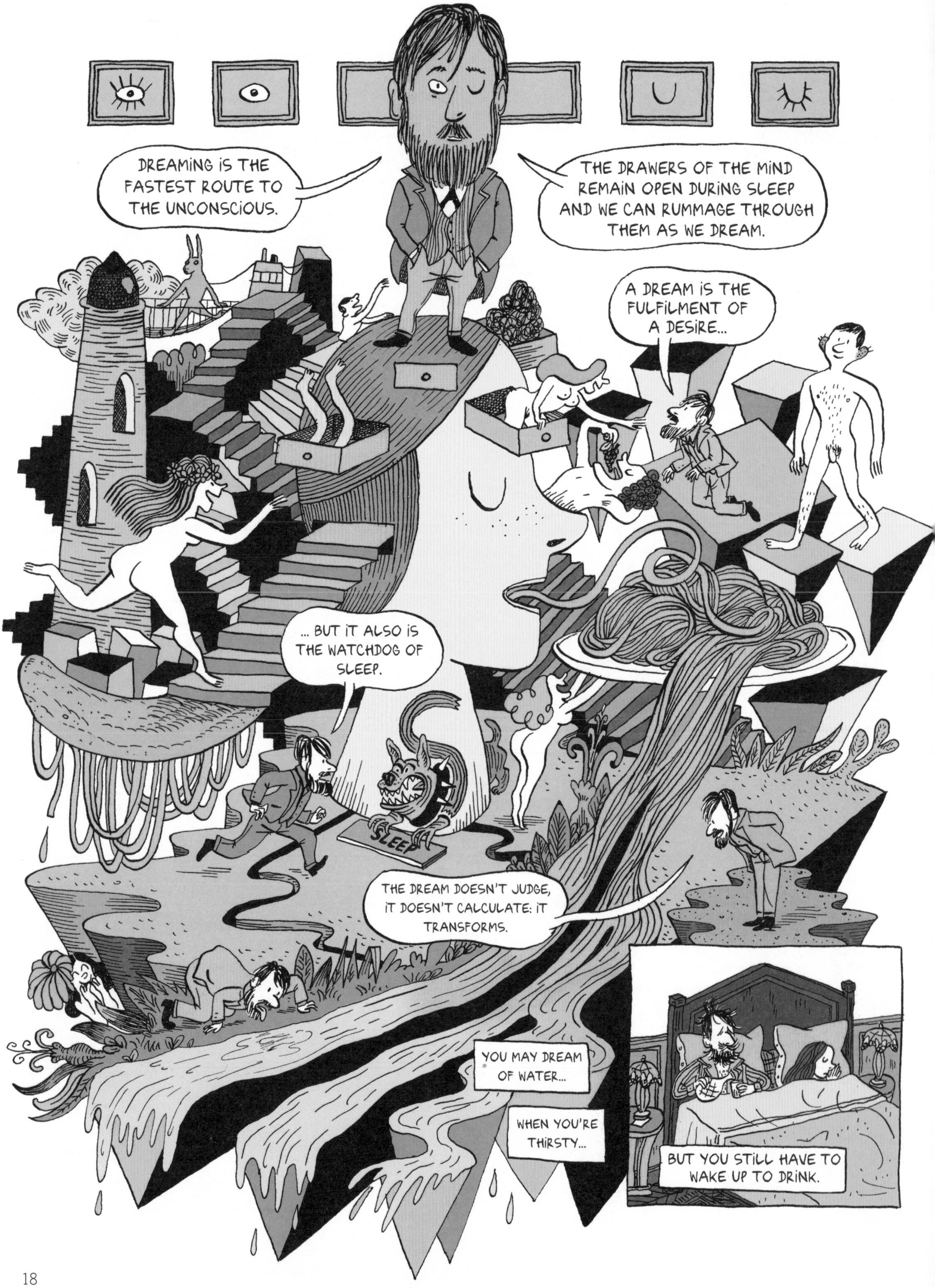
DREAMING IS THE FASTEST ROUTE TO THE UNCONSCIOUS.
THE DRAWERS OF THE MIND REMAIN OPEN DURING SLEEP AND WE CAN RUMMAGE THROUGH THEM AS WE DREAM.
A DREAM IS THE FULFILMENT OF A DESIRE...
... BUT IT ALSO IS THE WATCHDOG OF SLEEP.
SLEEP
THE DREAM DOESN'T JUDGE, IT DOESN'T CALCULATE: IT TRANSFORMS.
YOU MAY DREAM OF WATER...
WHEN YOU'RE THIRSTY...
BUT YOU STILL HAVE TO WAKE UP TO DRINK.

THE UNCONSCIOUS EXISTS! i MET IT.

THE PROOF?

ONE OF MY DREAMS.

IT'S ABOUT A JAB...

i dream that one of my patients, irma, suffers from a throat infection.

Rhaaa...

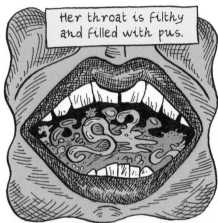

Her throat is filthy and filled with pus.

You're ill; it's your fault.

Rrrr

She was given a jab, but the needle must have been dirty.

RRRHH

CARAMBA!

WHAT DOES IT MEAN?

?

i HAVE A PASSION FOR CURING PEOPLE...

... TO GET TO THE BOTTOM OF THINGS.

IT'S NOT MY FAULT iF iRMA IS iLL.

This putrid mouth is the key to my dream: it's DEATH.

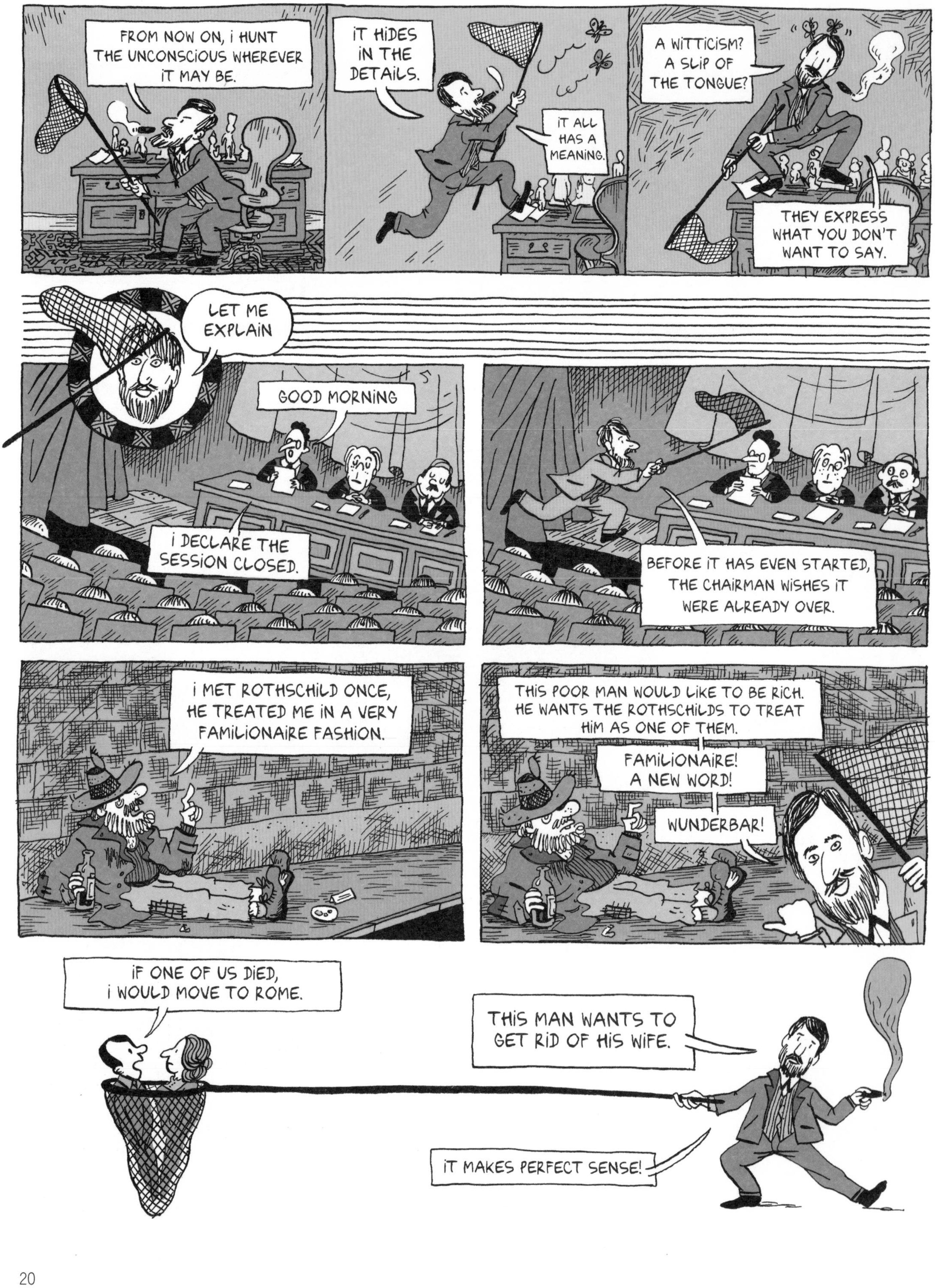
FROM NOW ON, I HUNT THE UNCONSCIOUS WHEREVER IT MAY BE.
IT HIDES IN THE DETAILS.
IT ALL HAS A MEANING.
A WITTICISM? A SLIP OF THE TONGUE?
THEY EXPRESS WHAT YOU DON'T WANT TO SAY.
LET ME EXPLAIN
GOOD MORNING
I DECLARE THE SESSION CLOSED.
BEFORE IT HAS EVEN STARTED, THE CHAIRMAN WISHES IT WERE ALREADY OVER.
I MET ROTHSCHILD ONCE, HE TREATED ME IN A VERY FAMILIONAIRE FASHION.
THIS POOR MAN WOULD LIKE TO BE RICH. HE WANTS THE ROTHSCHILDS TO TREAT HIM AS ONE OF THEM.
FAMILIONAIRE! A NEW WORD!
WUNDERBAR!
IF ONE OF US DIED, I WOULD MOVE TO ROME.
THIS MAN WANTS TO GET RID OF HIS WIFE.
IT MAKES PERFECT SENSE!

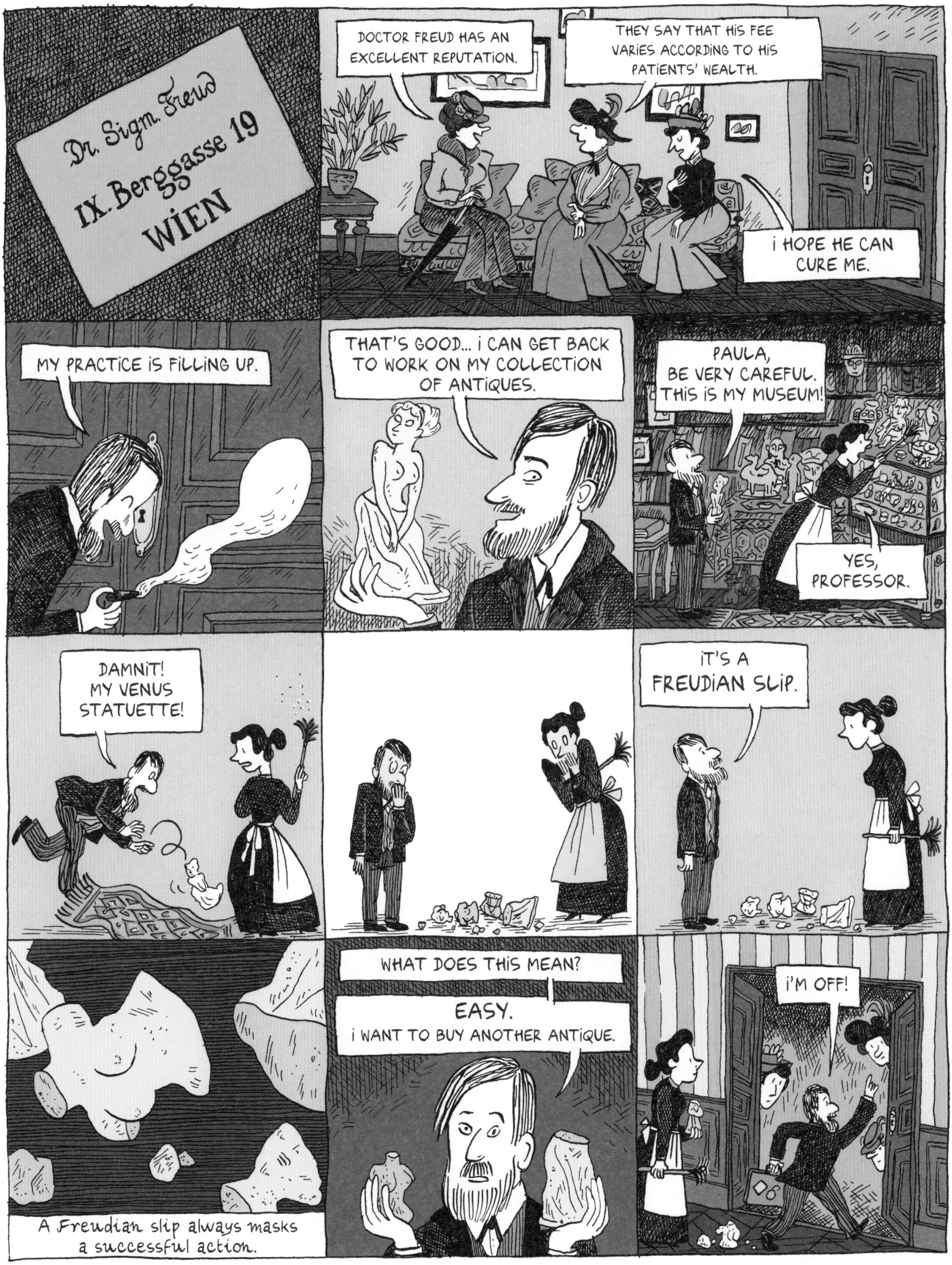
Dr. Sigm. Freud
IX. Berggasse 19
WIEN
DOCTOR FREUD HAS AN EXCELLENT REPUTATION.
THEY SAY THAT HIS FEE VARIES ACCORDING TO HIS PATIENTS' WEALTH.
I HOPE HE CAN CURE ME.
MY PRACTICE IS FILLING UP.
THAT'S GOOD... I CAN GET BACK TO WORK ON MY COLLECTION OF ANTIQUES.
PAULA, BE VERY CAREFUL. THIS IS MY MUSEUM!
YES, PROFESSOR.
DAMNIT! MY VENUS STATUETTE!
IT'S A FREUDIAN SLIP.
A Freudian slip always masks a successful action.
WHAT DOES THIS MEAN?
EASY. I WANT TO BUY ANOTHER ANTIQUE.
I'M OFF!

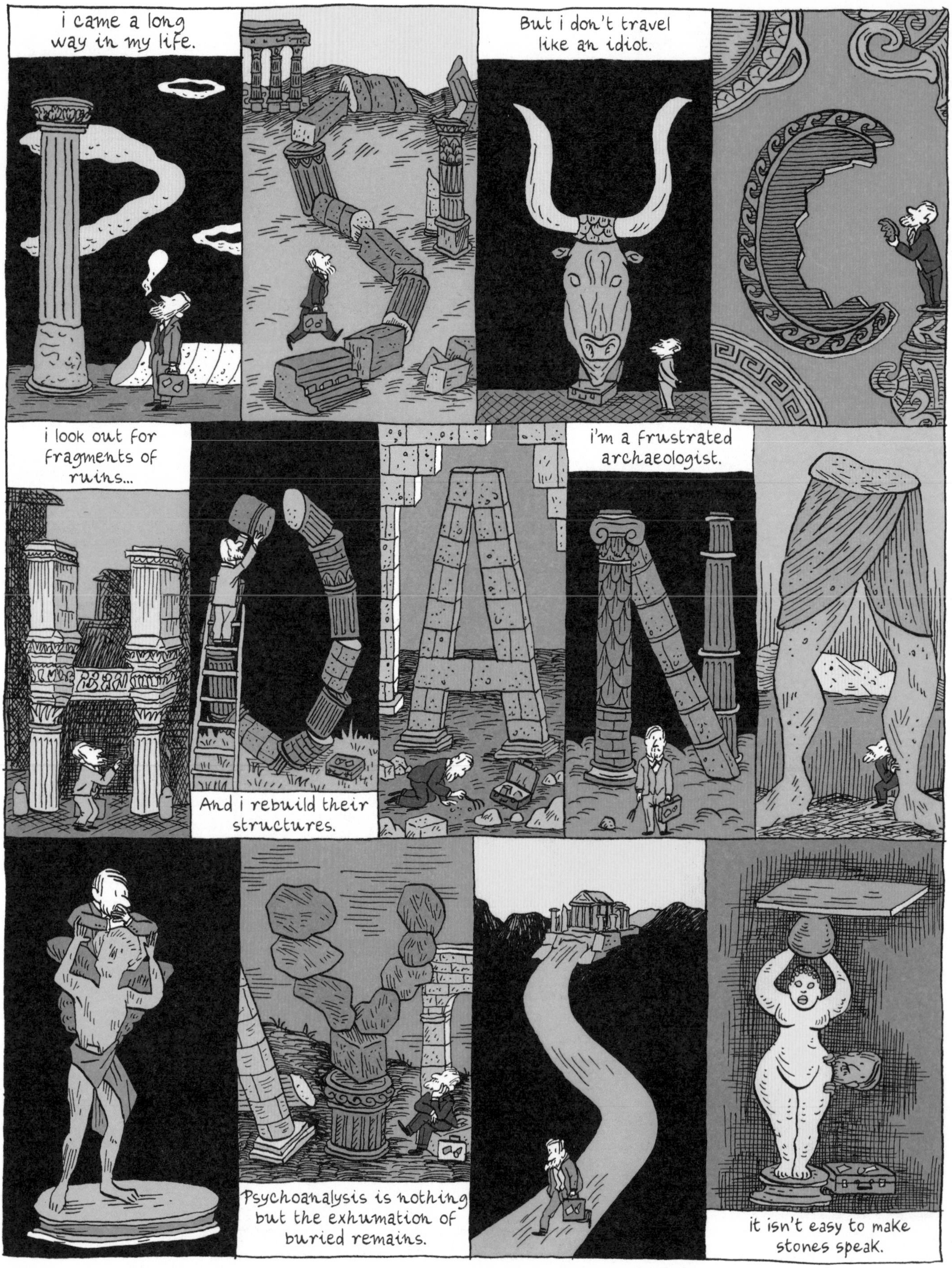
i came a long way in my life.
But i don't travel like an idiot.
i look out for fragments of ruins...
And i rebuild their structures.
i'm a frustrated archaeologist.
Psychoanalysis is nothing but the exhumation of buried remains.
it isn't easy to make stones speak.

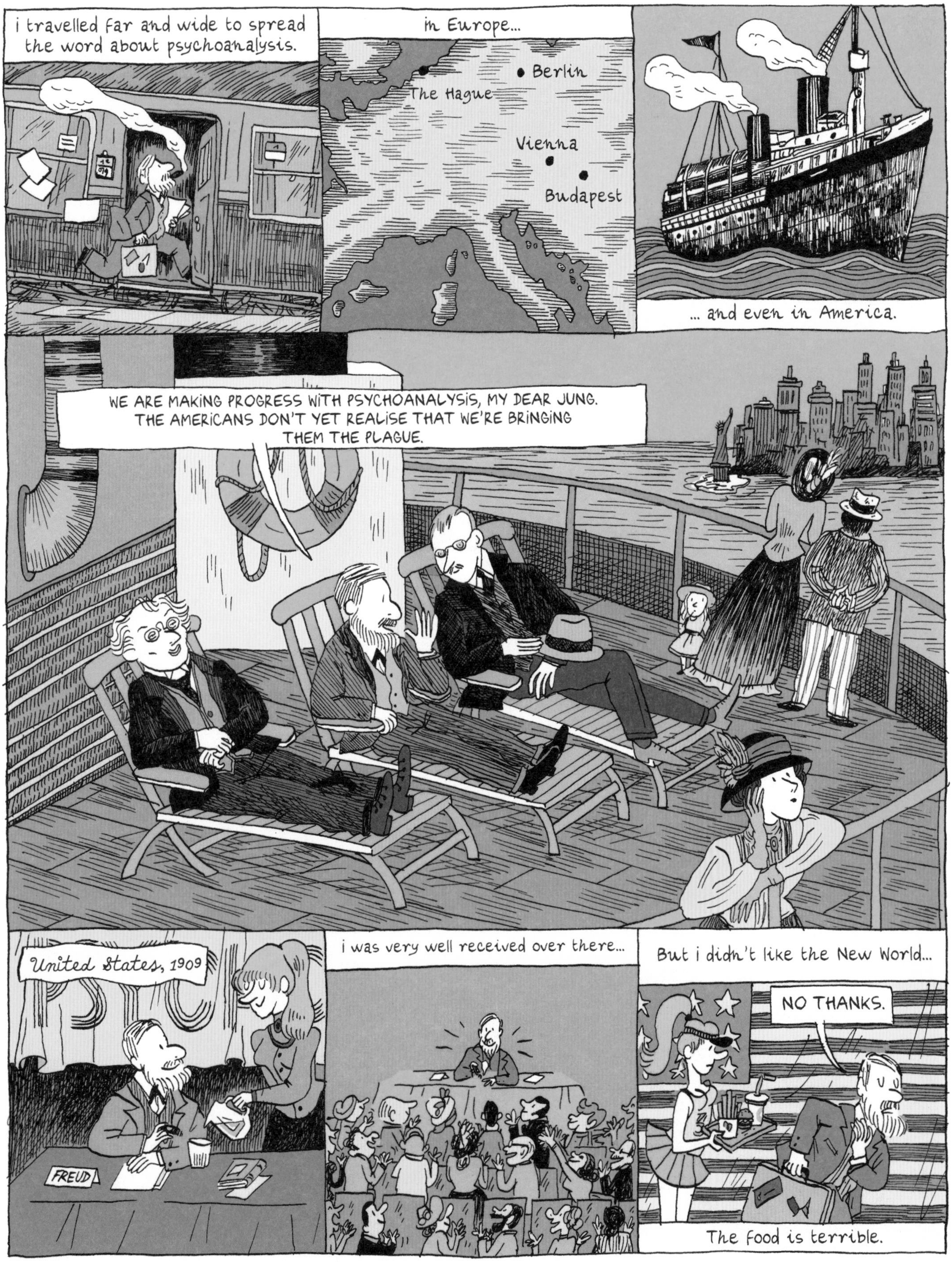
i travelled far and wide to spread the word about psychoanalysis.
in Europe...
Berlin
The Hague
Vienna
Budapest
... and even in America.
WE ARE MAKING PROGRESS WITH PSYCHOANALYSIS, MY DEAR JUNG. THE AMERICANS DON'T YET REALISE THAT WE'RE BRINGING THEM THE PLAGUE.
United States, 1909
FREUD
i was very well received over there...
But i didn't like the New World...
NO THANKS.
The food is terrible.

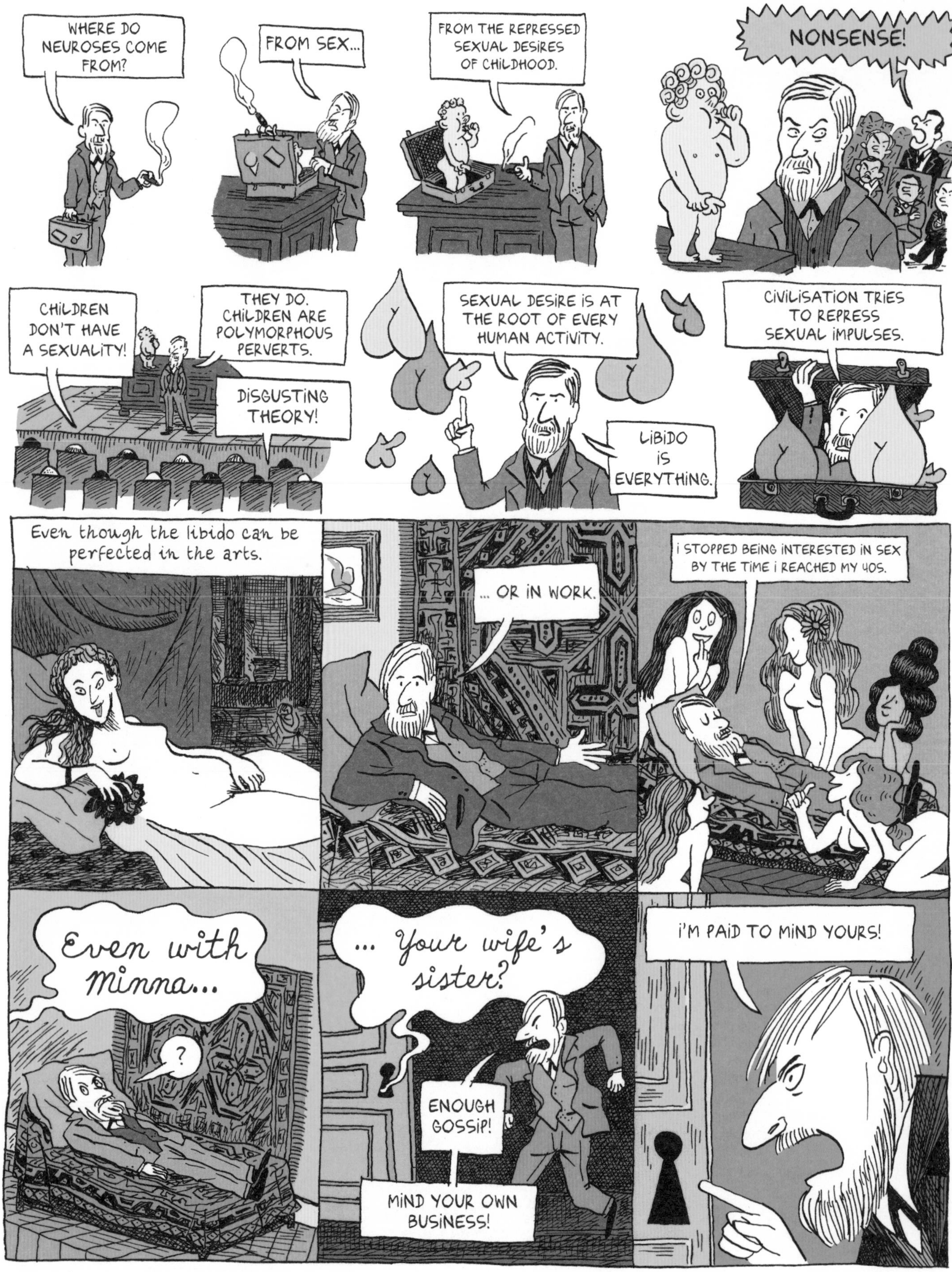
WHERE DO NEUROSES COME FROM?
FROM SEX...
FROM THE REPRESSED SEXUAL DESIRES OF CHILDHOOD.
NONSENSE!
CHILDREN DON'T HAVE A SEXUALITY!
THEY DO. CHILDREN ARE POLYMORPHOUS PERVERTS.
DISGUSTING THEORY!
SEXUAL DESIRE IS AT THE ROOT OF EVERY HUMAN ACTIVITY.
LIBIDO IS EVERYTHING.
CIVILISATION TRIES TO REPRESS SEXUAL IMPULSES.
Even though the libido can be perfected in the arts.
... OR IN WORK.
I STOPPED BEING INTERESTED IN SEX BY THE TIME I REACHED MY 40S.
Even with Minna...
?
... Your wife's sister?
ENOUGH GOSSIP!
MIND YOUR OWN BUSINESS!
I'M PAID TO MIND YOURS!

The DORA Case

MY NAME IS DORA.

i'M HERE BECAUSE MY FATHER FORCED ME TO COME.

MY PARENTS ... COFF COFF COFF!

RRR... SOZ!

MY PARENTS HAVE THESE FRIENDS, THE K FAMILY.

MY FATHER SLEEPS WITH MRS. K.

WELL, «SLEEPS»...

BWEURRR... COFF!

i DON'T KNOW WHAT THEY DO EXACTLY.

MY FATHER iS iLL AND iMPOTENT.

MR. K WANTS TO BE WITH ME. HE TRIED TO KiSS ME ONE EVENING. iT REALLY PiSSED ME OFF!

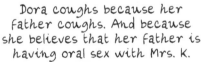

Dora coughs because her father coughs. And because she believes that her father is having oral sex with Mrs. K.

MR. K. iS QUITE ATTRACTIVE, iSN'T HE?

WOULDN'T YOU LiKE TO MARRY HiM?

?!?

YOU'RE ANNOYING ME!

i'M OUTTA HERE!

GOODBYE!

NO!

i FEEL LiKE i'M MiSSiNG SOMETHING.

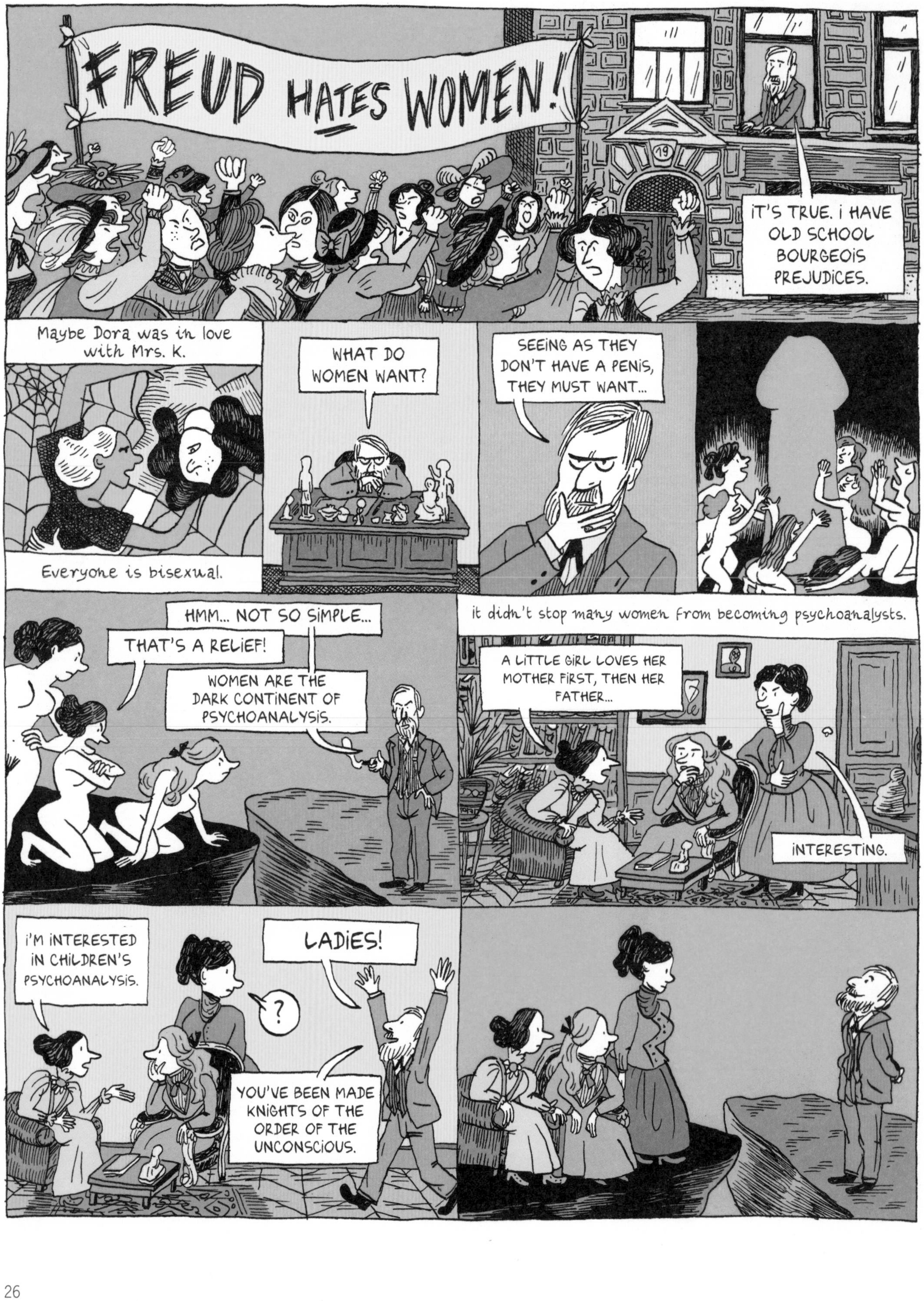
FREUD HATES WOMEN!
IT'S TRUE. I HAVE OLD SCHOOL BOURGEOIS PREJUDICES.
Maybe Dora was in love with Mrs. K.
Everyone is bisexual.
WHAT DO WOMEN WANT?
SEEING AS THEY DON'T HAVE A PENIS, THEY MUST WANT...
HMM... NOT SO SIMPLE...
THAT'S A RELIEF!
WOMEN ARE THE DARK CONTINENT OF PSYCHOANALYSIS.
it didn't stop many women from becoming psychoanalysts.
A LITTLE GIRL LOVES HER MOTHER FIRST, THEN HER FATHER...
INTERESTING.
I'M INTERESTED IN CHILDREN'S PSYCHOANALYSIS.
?
LADIES!
YOU'VE BEEN MADE KNIGHTS OF THE ORDER OF THE UNCONSCIOUS.

The Oedipus Complex

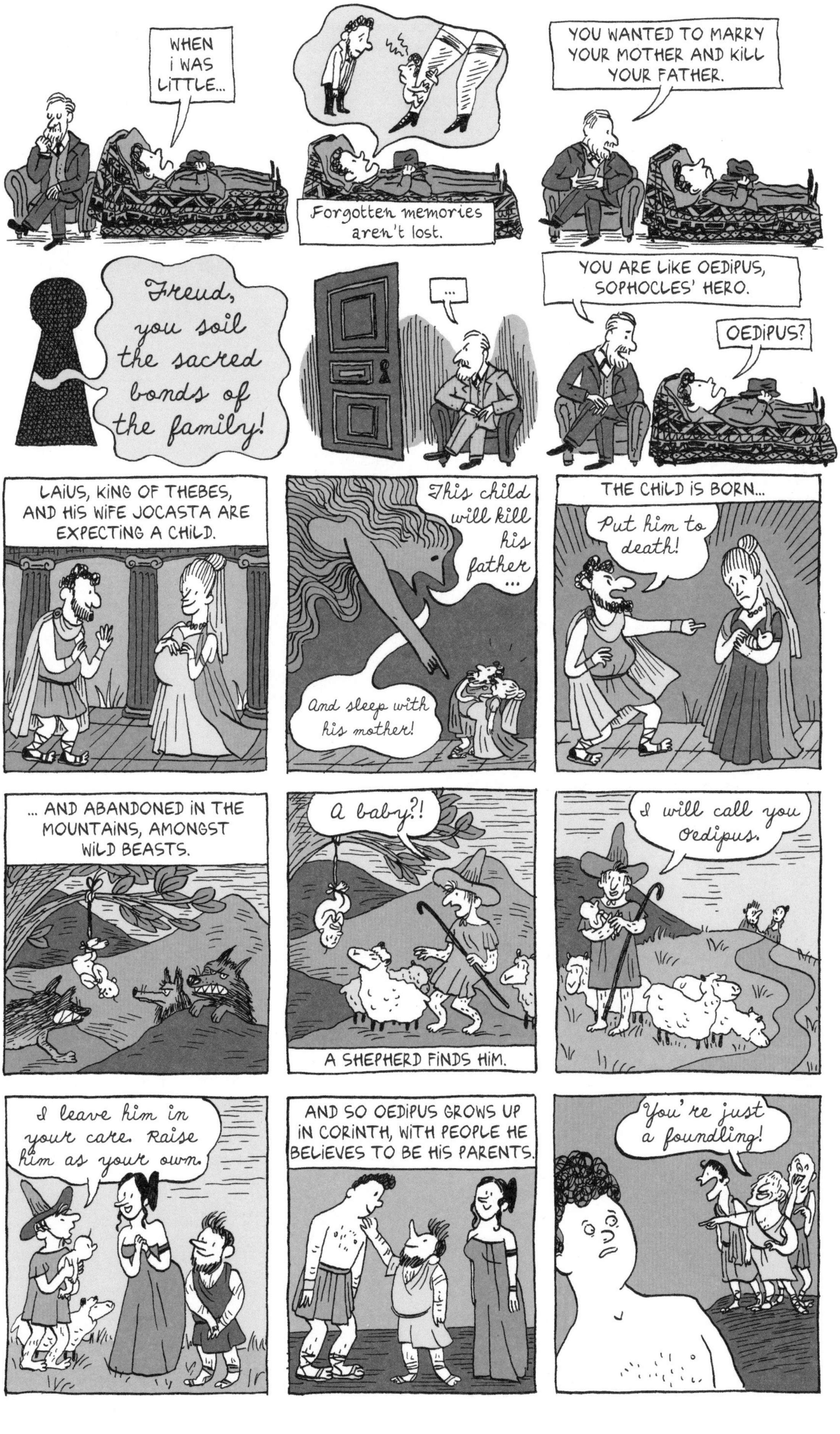
WHEN I WAS LITTLE...
Forgotten memories aren't lost.
YOU WANTED TO MARRY YOUR MOTHER AND KILL YOUR FATHER.
Freud, you soil the sacred bonds of the family!
...
YOU ARE LIKE OEDIPUS, SOPHOCLES' HERO.
OEDIPUS?
LAIUS, KING OF THEBES, AND HIS WIFE JOCASTA ARE EXPECTING A CHILD.
This child will kill his father...
And sleep with his mother!
THE CHILD IS BORN...
Put him to death!
... AND ABANDONED IN THE MOUNTAINS, AMONGST WILD BEASTS.
A baby?!
A SHEPHERD FINDS HIM.
I will call you Oedipus.
I leave him in your care. Raise him as your own.
AND SO OEDIPUS GROWS UP IN CORINTH, WITH PEOPLE HE BELIEVES TO BE HIS PARENTS.
You're just a foundling!

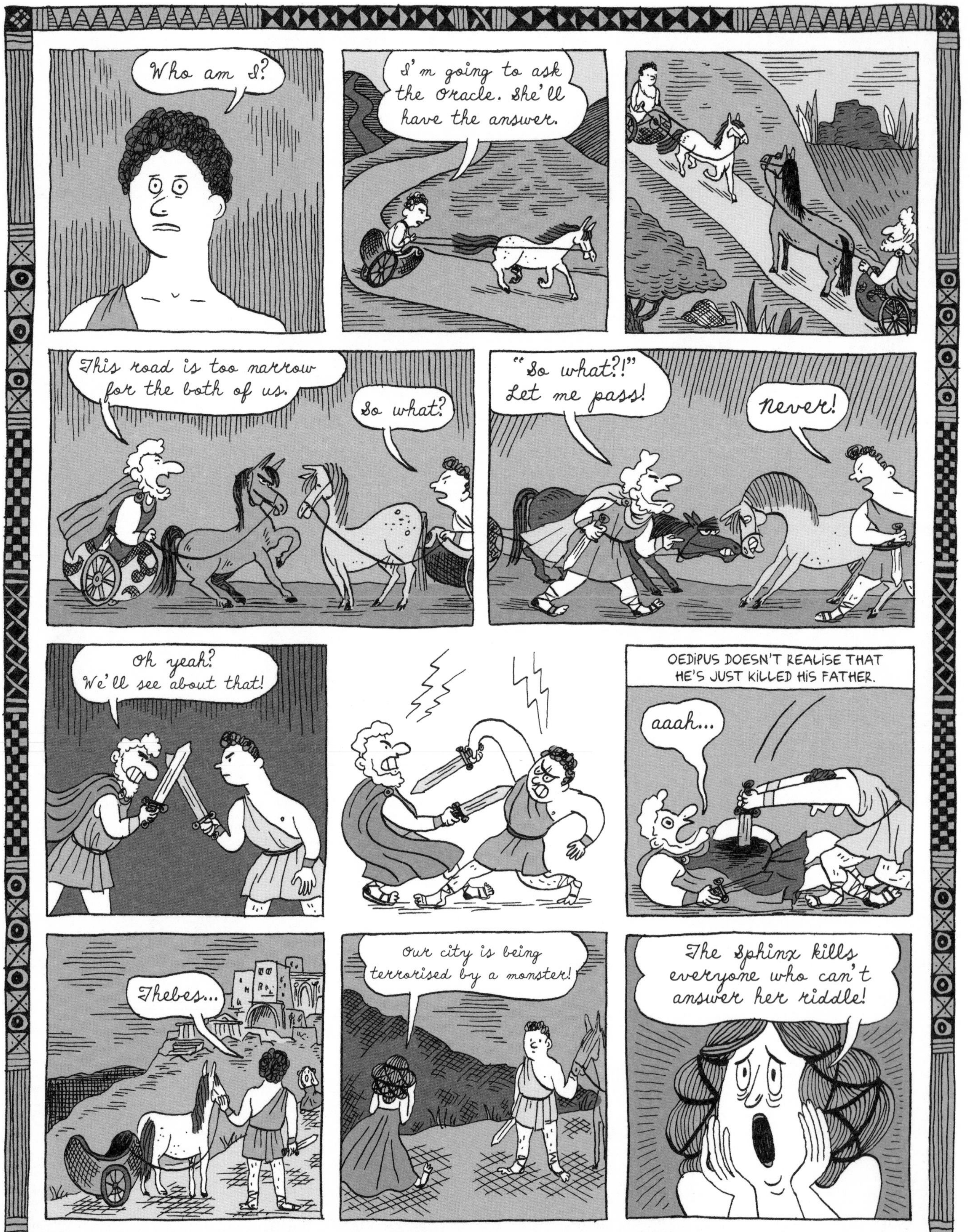

Who am I?
I'm going to ask the Oracle. She'll have the answer.
This road is too narrow for the both of us.
So what?
"So what?!" Let me pass!
Never!
Oh yeah? We'll see about that!
OEDIPUS DOESN'T REALISE THAT HE'S JUST KILLED HIS FATHER.
aaah...
Thebes...
Our city is being terrorised by a monster!
The Sphinx kills everyone who can't answer her riddle!

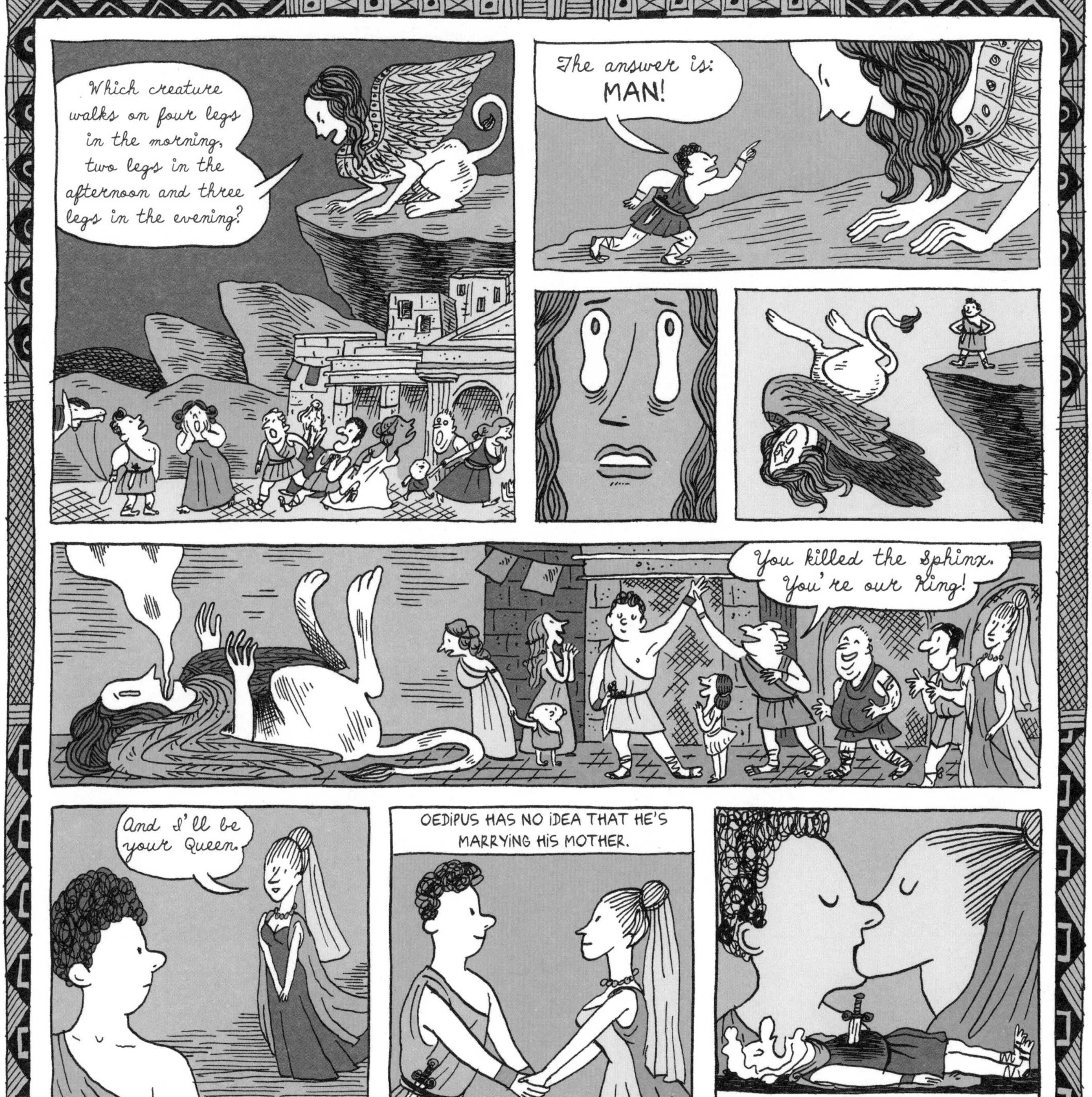
Which creature walks on four legs in the morning, two legs in the afternoon and three legs in the evening?
The answer is: MAN!
You killed the Sphinx. You're our King!
And I'll be your Queen.
OEDIPUS HAS NO IDEA THAT HE'S MARRYING HIS MOTHER.
AND THUS THE PROPHECY COMES TRUE.

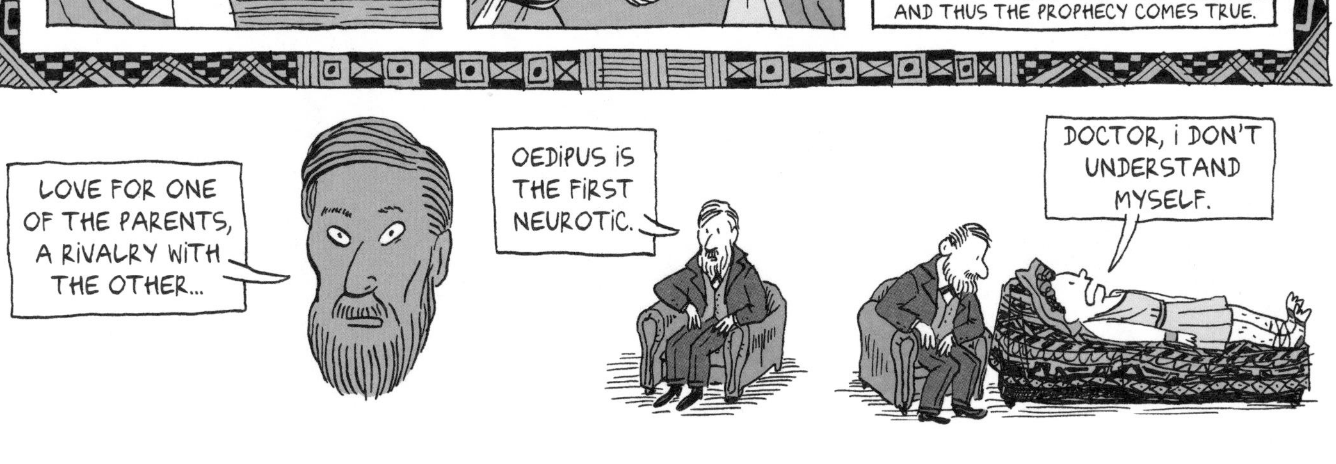
LOVE FOR ONE OF THE PARENTS, A RIVALRY WITH THE OTHER...
OEDIPUS IS THE FIRST NEUROTIC.
DOCTOR, I DON'T UNDERSTAND MYSELF.

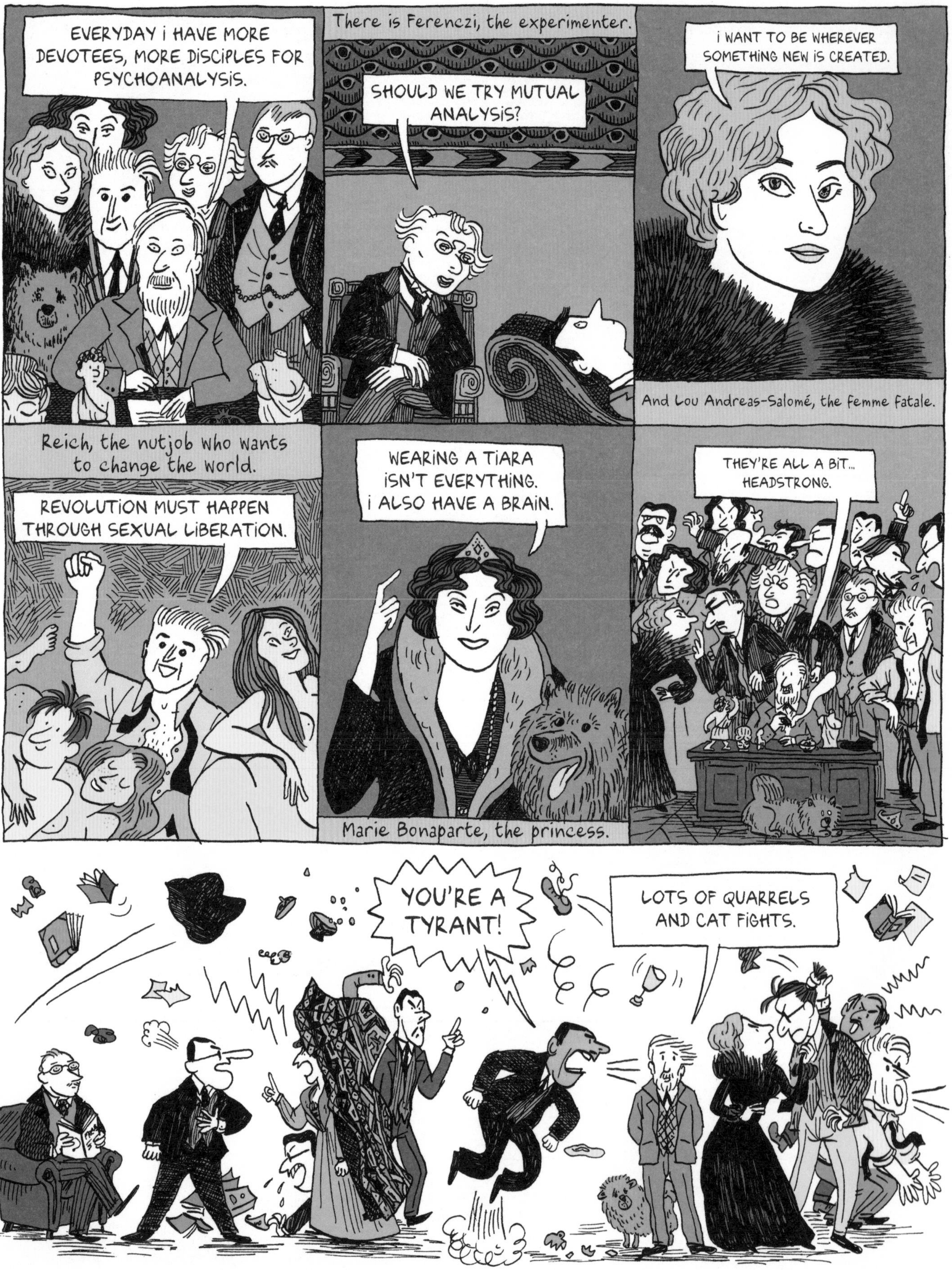
EVERYDAY I HAVE MORE DEVOTEES, MORE DISCIPLES FOR PSYCHOANALYSIS.
There is Ferenczi, the experimenter.
SHOULD WE TRY MUTUAL ANALYSIS?
I WANT TO BE WHEREVER SOMETHING NEW IS CREATED.
And Lou Andreas-Salomé, the femme fatale.
Reich, the nutjob who wants to change the world.
REVOLUTION MUST HAPPEN THROUGH SEXUAL LIBERATION.
WEARING A TIARA ISN'T EVERYTHING. I ALSO HAVE A BRAIN.
Marie Bonaparte, the princess.
THEY'RE ALL A BIT... HEADSTRONG.
YOU'RE A TYRANT!
LOTS OF QUARRELS AND CAT FIGHTS.

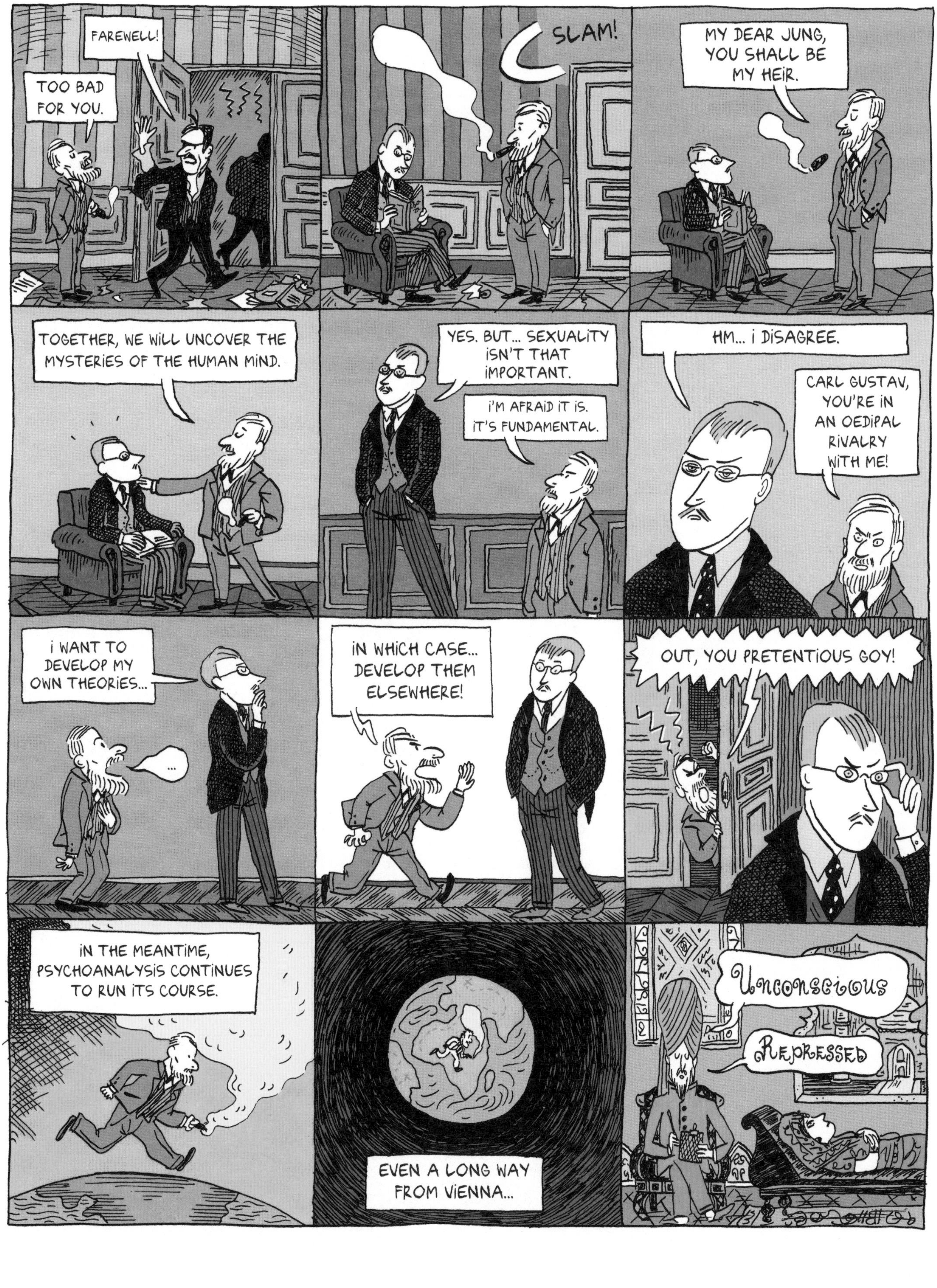
FAREWELL!
TOO BAD FOR YOU.
SLAM!
MY DEAR JUNG, YOU SHALL BE MY HEIR.
TOGETHER, WE WILL UNCOVER THE MYSTERIES OF THE HUMAN MIND.
YES. BUT... SEXUALITY ISN'T THAT IMPORTANT.
I'M AFRAID IT IS. IT'S FUNDAMENTAL.
HM... I DISAGREE.
CARL GUSTAV, YOU'RE IN AN OEDIPAL RIVALRY WITH ME!
I WANT TO DEVELOP MY OWN THEORIES...
...
IN WHICH CASE... DEVELOP THEM ELSEWHERE!
OUT, YOU PRETENTIOUS GOY!
IN THE MEANTIME, PSYCHOANALYSIS CONTINUES TO RUN ITS COURSE.
EVEN A LONG WAY FROM VIENNA...
Unconscious
Repressed

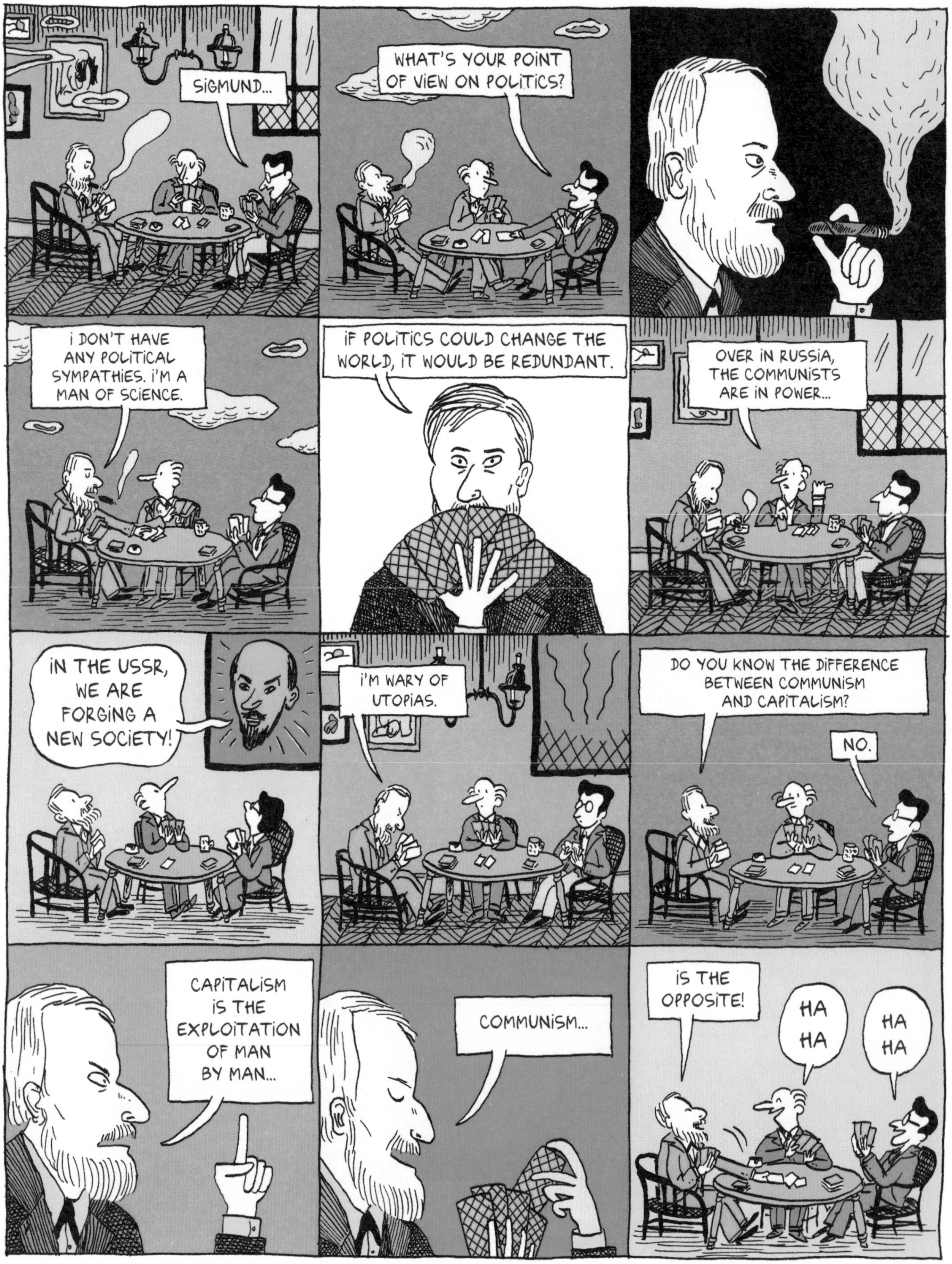

SIGMUND...
WHAT'S YOUR POINT OF VIEW ON POLITICS?
I DON'T HAVE ANY POLITICAL SYMPATHIES. I'M A MAN OF SCIENCE.
IF POLITICS COULD CHANGE THE WORLD, IT WOULD BE REDUNDANT.
OVER IN RUSSIA, THE COMMUNISTS ARE IN POWER...
IN THE USSR, WE ARE FORGING A NEW SOCIETY!
I'M WARY OF UTOPIAS.
DO YOU KNOW THE DIFFERENCE BETWEEN COMMUNISM AND CAPITALISM?
NO.
CAPITALISM IS THE EXPLOITATION OF MAN BY MAN...
COMMUNISM...
IS THE OPPOSITE!
HA HA
HA HA

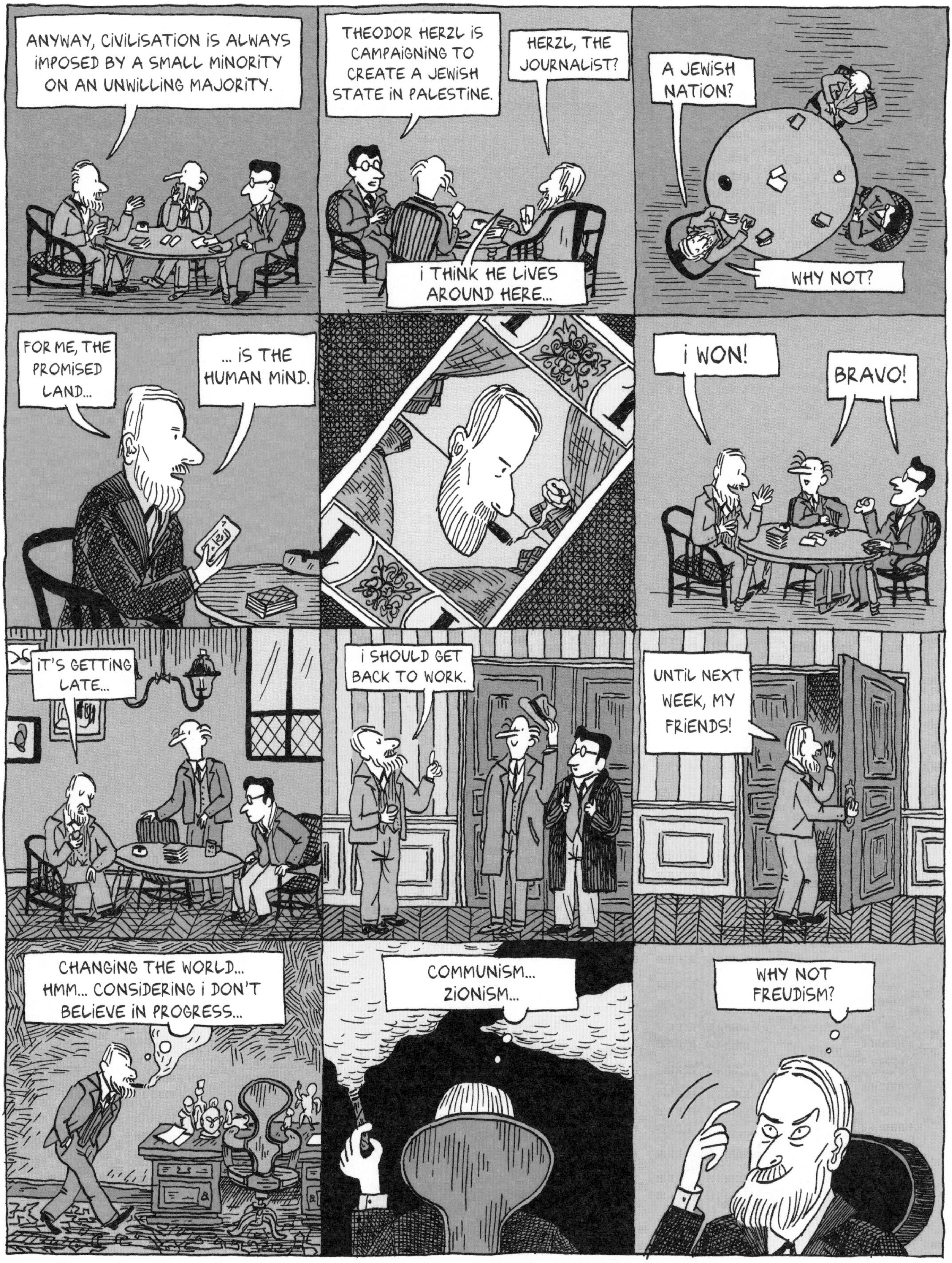
ANYWAY, CIVILISATION IS ALWAYS IMPOSED BY A SMALL MINORITY ON AN UNWILLING MAJORITY.
THEODOR HERZL IS CAMPAIGNING TO CREATE A JEWISH STATE IN PALESTINE.
HERZL, THE JOURNALIST?
I THINK HE LIVES AROUND HERE...
A JEWISH NATION?
WHY NOT?
FOR ME, THE PROMISED LAND...
... IS THE HUMAN MIND.
I WON!
BRAVO!
IT'S GETTING LATE...
I SHOULD GET BACK TO WORK.
UNTIL NEXT WEEK, MY FRIENDS!
CHANGING THE WORLD... HMM... CONSIDERING I DON'T BELIEVE IN PROGRESS...
COMMUNISM... ZIONISM...
WHY NOT FREUDISM?

THE CASE OF THE RAT MAN

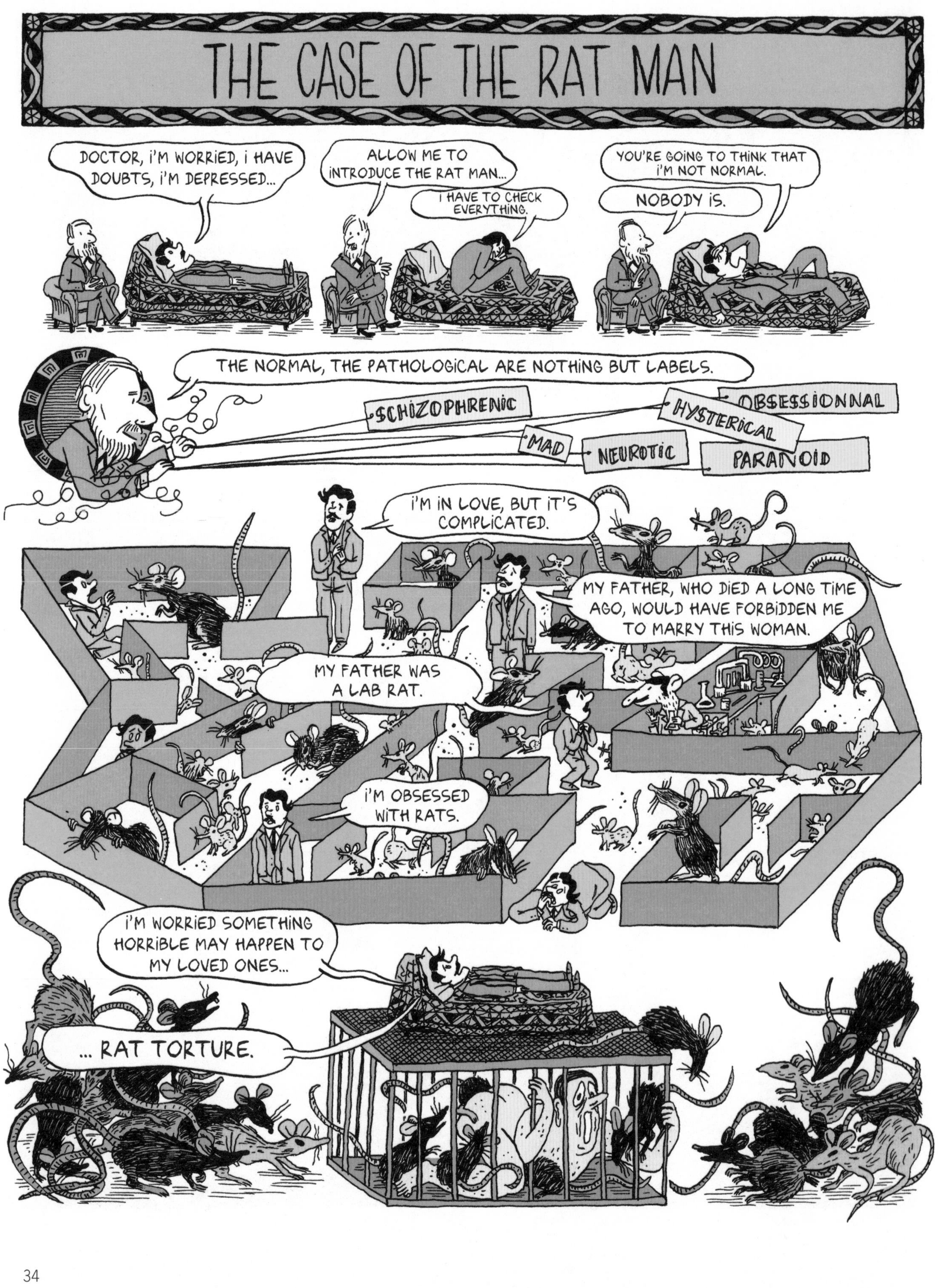
DOCTOR, I'M WORRIED, I HAVE DOUBTS, I'M DEPRESSED...
ALLOW ME TO INTRODUCE THE RAT MAN...
I HAVE TO CHECK EVERYTHING.
YOU'RE GOING TO THINK THAT I'M NOT NORMAL.
NOBODY IS.
THE NORMAL, THE PATHOLOGICAL ARE NOTHING BUT LABELS.
SCHIZOPHRENIC
OBSESSIONNAL
HYSTERICAL
MAD
NEUROTIC
PARANOID
I'M IN LOVE, BUT IT'S COMPLICATED.
MY FATHER, WHO DIED A LONG TIME AGO, WOULD HAVE FORBIDDEN ME TO MARRY THIS WOMAN.
MY FATHER WAS A LAB RAT.
I'M OBSESSED WITH RATS.
I'M WORRIED SOMETHING HORRIBLE MAY HAPPEN TO MY LOVED ONES...
... RAT TORTURE.

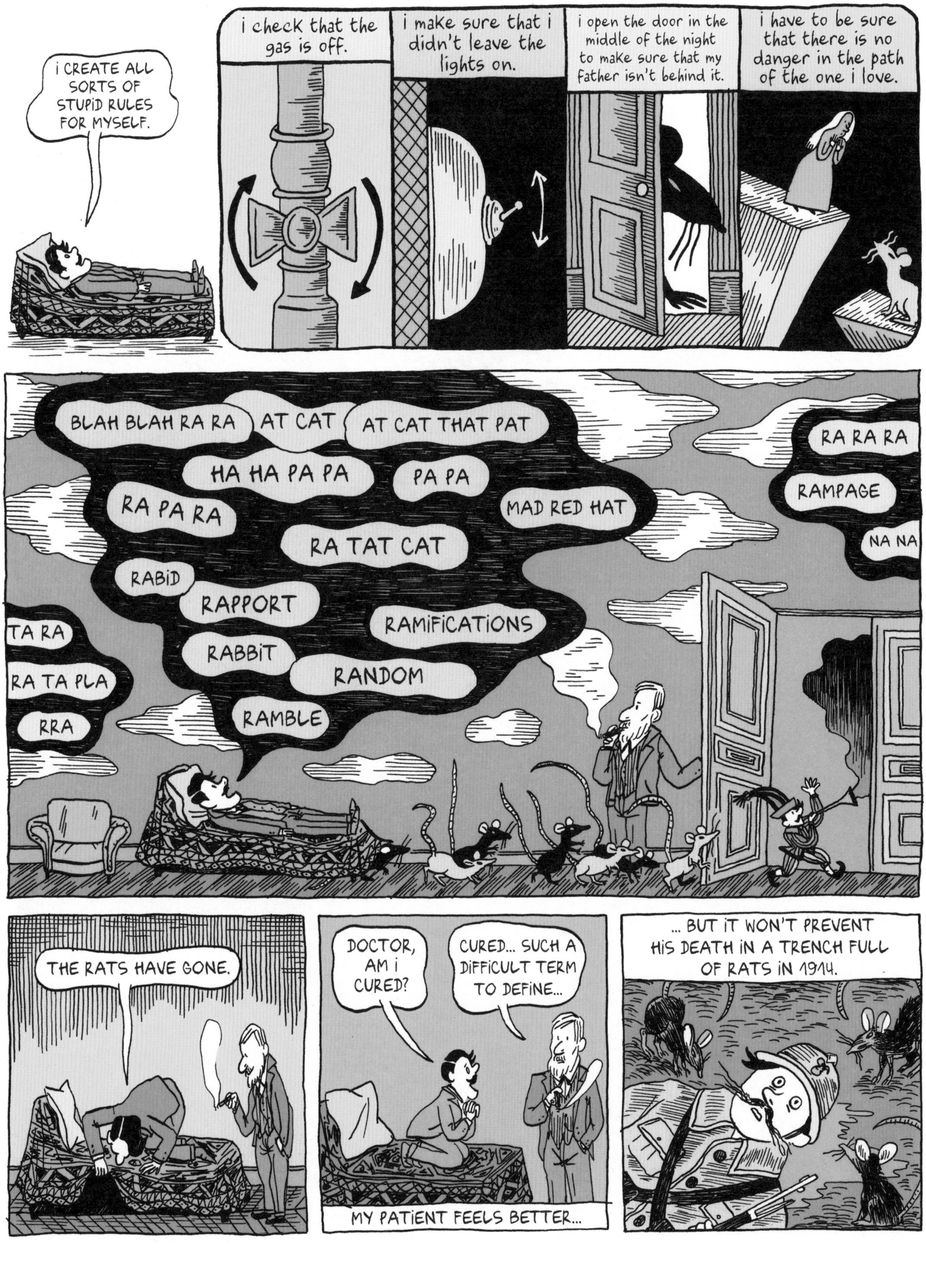

i CREATE ALL SORTS OF STUPiD RULES FOR MYSELF.
i check that the gas is off.
i make sure that i didn't leave the lights on.
i open the door in the middle of the night to make sure that my father isn't behind it.
i have to be sure that there is no danger in the path of the one i love.
BLAH BLAH RA RA
AT CAT
AT CAT THAT PAT
HA HA PA PA
PA PA
RA PA RA
MAD RED HAT
RA TAT CAT
RABiD
RAPPORT
RAMiFiCATiONS
RABBiT
RANDOM
RAMBLE
TA RA
RA TA PLA
RRA
RA RA RA
RAMPAGE
NA NA
THE RATS HAVE GONE.
DOCTOR, AM i CURED?
CURED... SUCH A DiFFiCULT TERM TO DEFiNE...
MY PATiENT FEELS BETTER...
... BUT iT WON'T PREVENT HiS DEATH iN A TRENCH FULL OF RATS iN 1914.

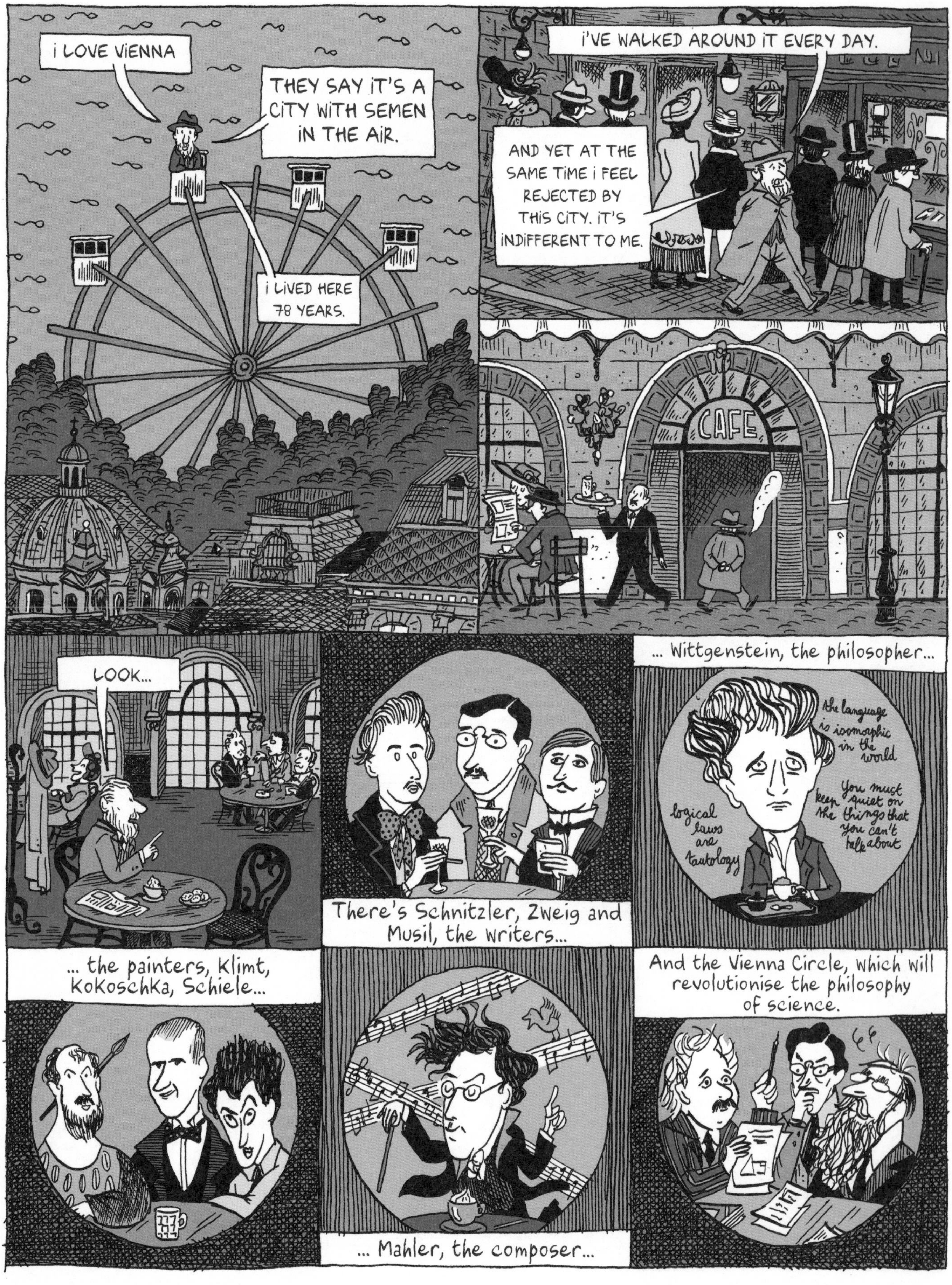

i LOVE ViENNA
THEY SAY iT'S A CiTY WiTH SEMEN iN THE AiR.
i LiVED HERE 78 YEARS.
i'VE WALKED AROUND iT EVERY DAY.
AND YET AT THE SAME TiME i FEEL REJECTED BY THiS CiTY. iT'S iNDiFFERENT TO ME.
CAFE
LOOK...
There's Schnitzler, Zweig and Musil, the writers...
... Wittgenstein, the philosopher...
the language is isomorphic in the world
You must keep quiet on the things that you can't talk about
logical laws are tautology
... the painters, Klimt, KoKoschKa, Schiele...
... Mahler, the composer...
And the Vienna Circle, which will revolutionise the philosophy of science.

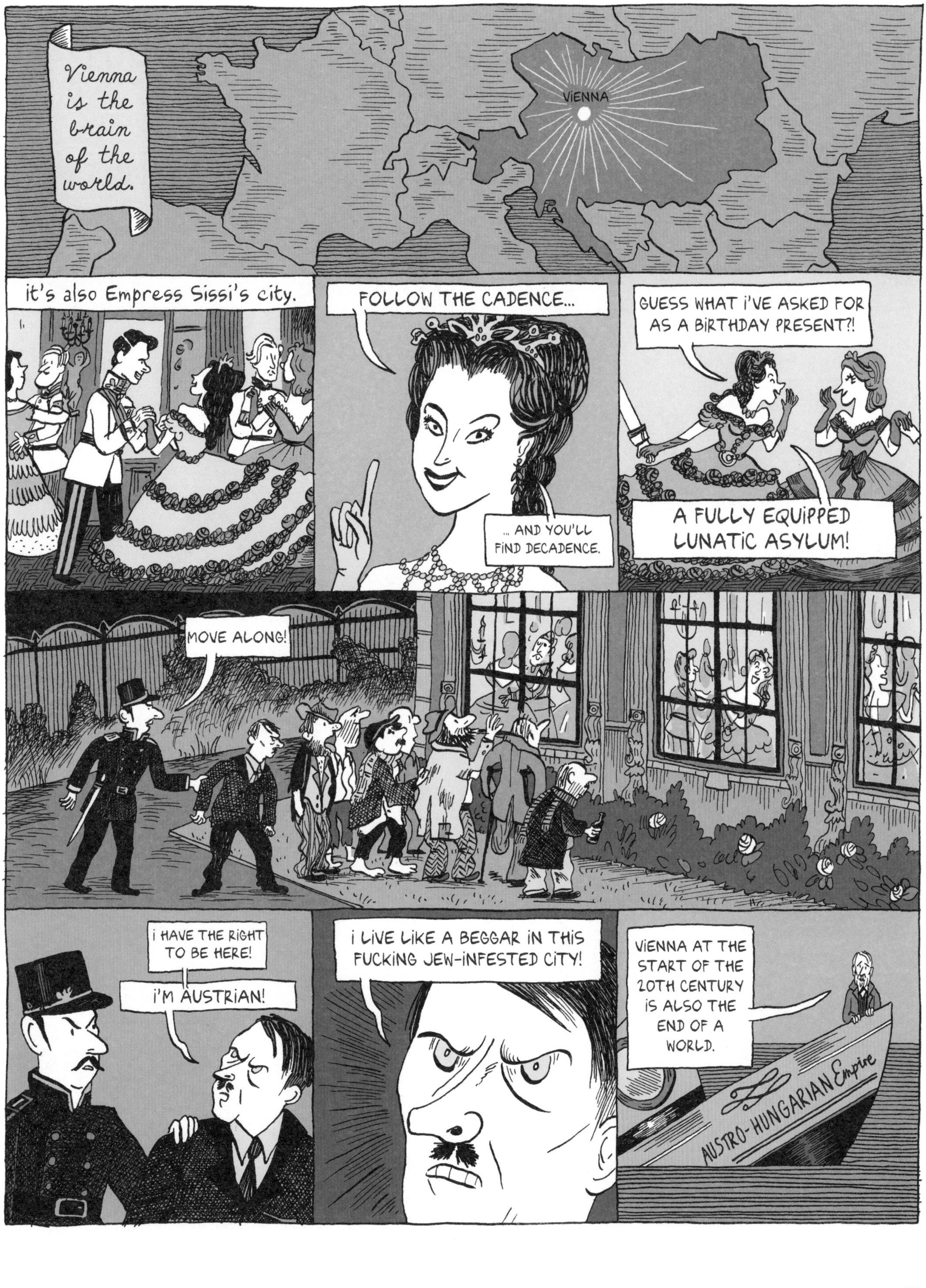
Vienna is the brain of the world.
VIENNA
it's also Empress Sissi's city.
FOLLOW THE CADENCE...
... AND YOU'LL FIND DECADENCE.
GUESS WHAT I'VE ASKED FOR AS A BIRTHDAY PRESENT?!
A FULLY EQUIPPED LUNATIC ASYLUM!
MOVE ALONG!
I HAVE THE RIGHT TO BE HERE!
I'M AUSTRIAN!
I LIVE LIKE A BEGGAR IN THIS FUCKING JEW-INFESTED CITY!
VIENNA AT THE START OF THE 20TH CENTURY IS ALSO THE END OF A WORLD.
AUSTRO-HUNGARIAN Empire

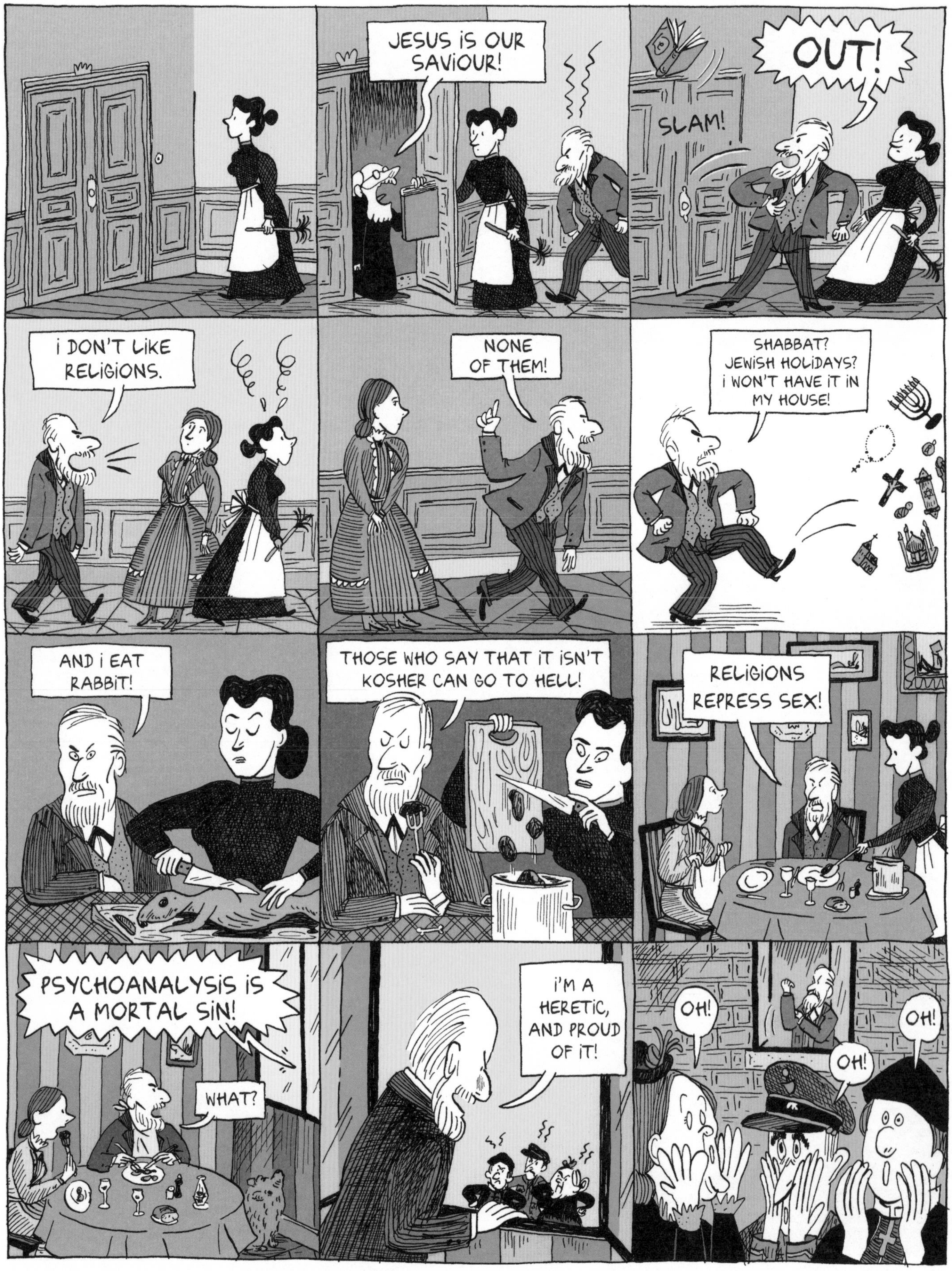
JESUS IS OUR SAVIOUR!
SLAM!
OUT!
I DON'T LIKE RELIGIONS.
NONE OF THEM!
SHABBAT? JEWISH HOLIDAYS? I WON'T HAVE IT IN MY HOUSE!
AND I EAT RABBIT!
THOSE WHO SAY THAT IT ISN'T KOSHER CAN GO TO HELL!
RELIGIONS REPRESS SEX!
PSYCHOANALYSIS IS A MORTAL SIN!
WHAT?
I'M A HERETIC, AND PROUD OF IT!
OH!
OH!
OH!

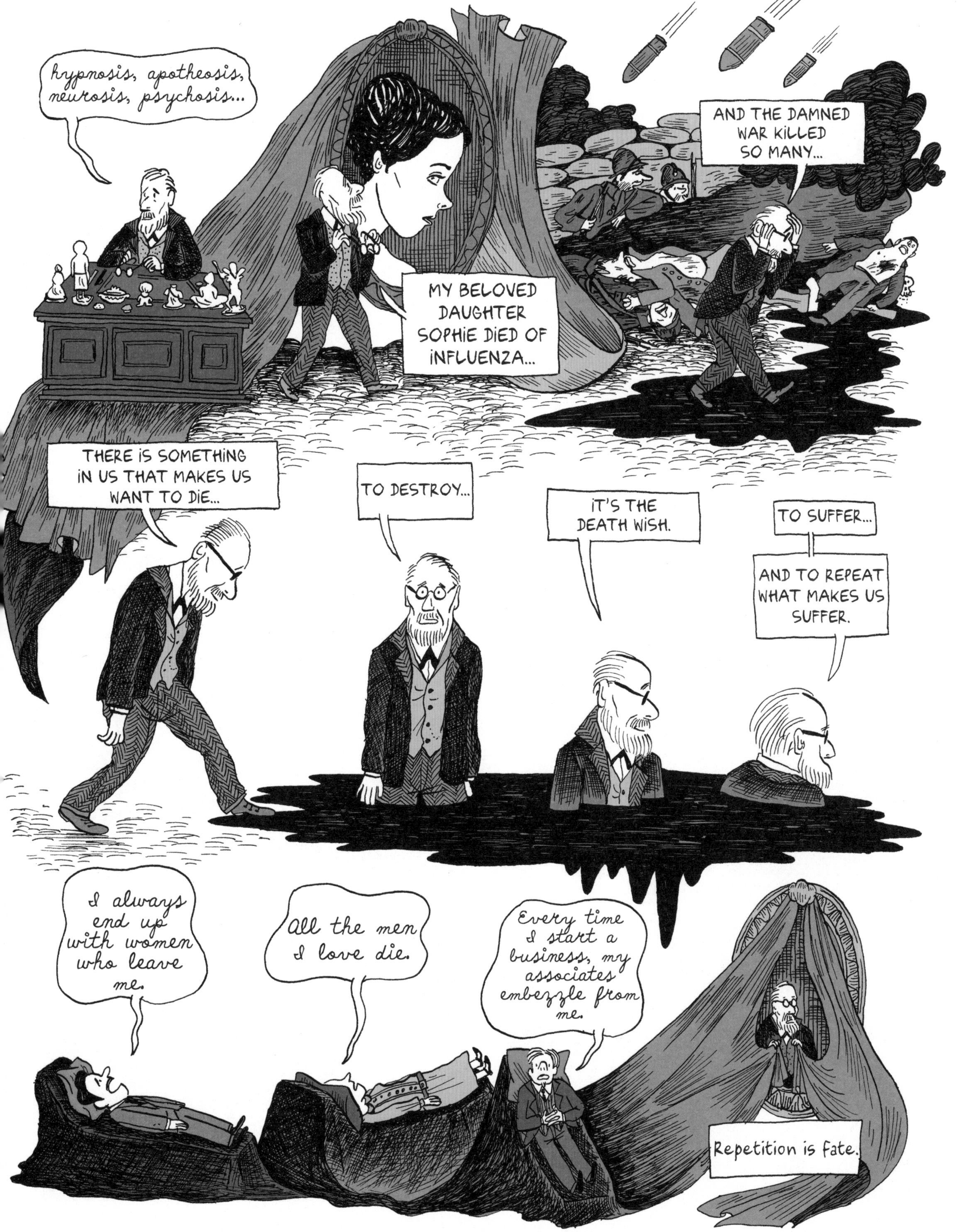
hypnosis, apotheosis, neurosis, psychosis...
MY BELOVED DAUGHTER SOPHIE DIED OF INFLUENZA...
AND THE DAMNED WAR KILLED SO MANY...
THERE IS SOMETHING IN US THAT MAKES US WANT TO DIE...
TO DESTROY...
IT'S THE DEATH WISH.
TO SUFFER...
AND TO REPEAT WHAT MAKES US SUFFER.
I always end up with women who leave me.
All the men I love die.
Every time I start a business, my associates embezzle from me.
Repetition is fate.

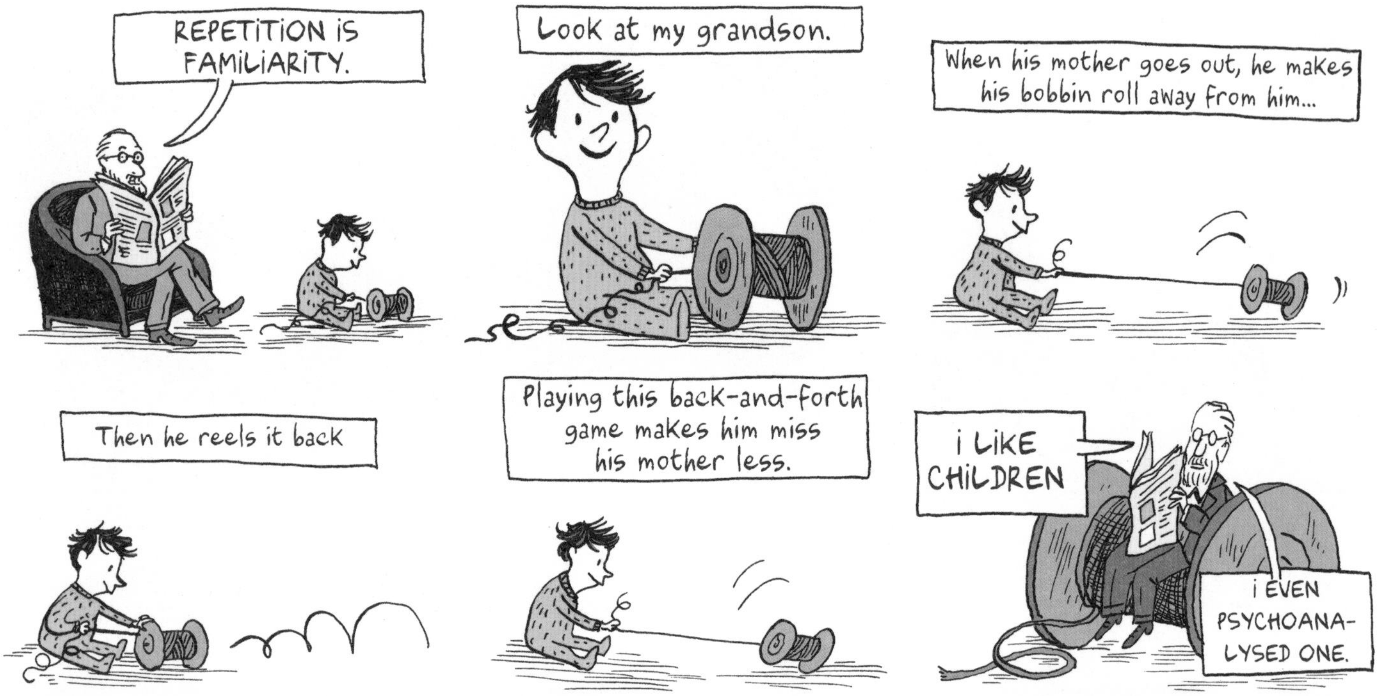
REPETITION IS FAMILIARITY.
Look at my grandson.
When his mother goes out, he makes his bobbin roll away from him...
Then he reels it back
Playing this back-and-forth game makes him miss his mother less.
I LIKE CHILDREN
I EVEN PSYCHOANA-LYSED ONE.

THE CASE OF LITTLE HANS

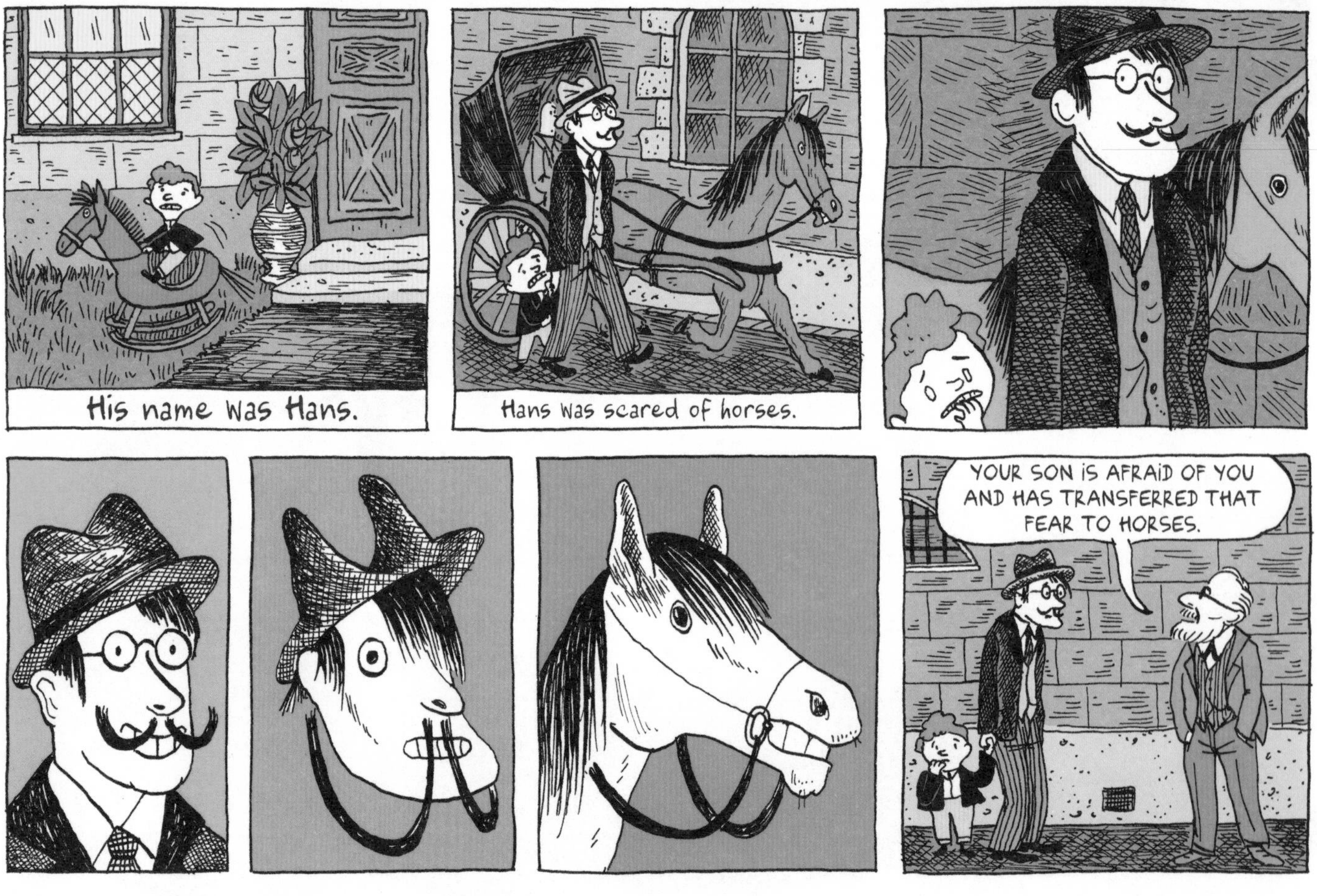
His name was Hans.
Hans was scared of horses.
YOUR SON IS AFRAID OF YOU AND HAS TRANSFERRED THAT FEAR TO HORSES.

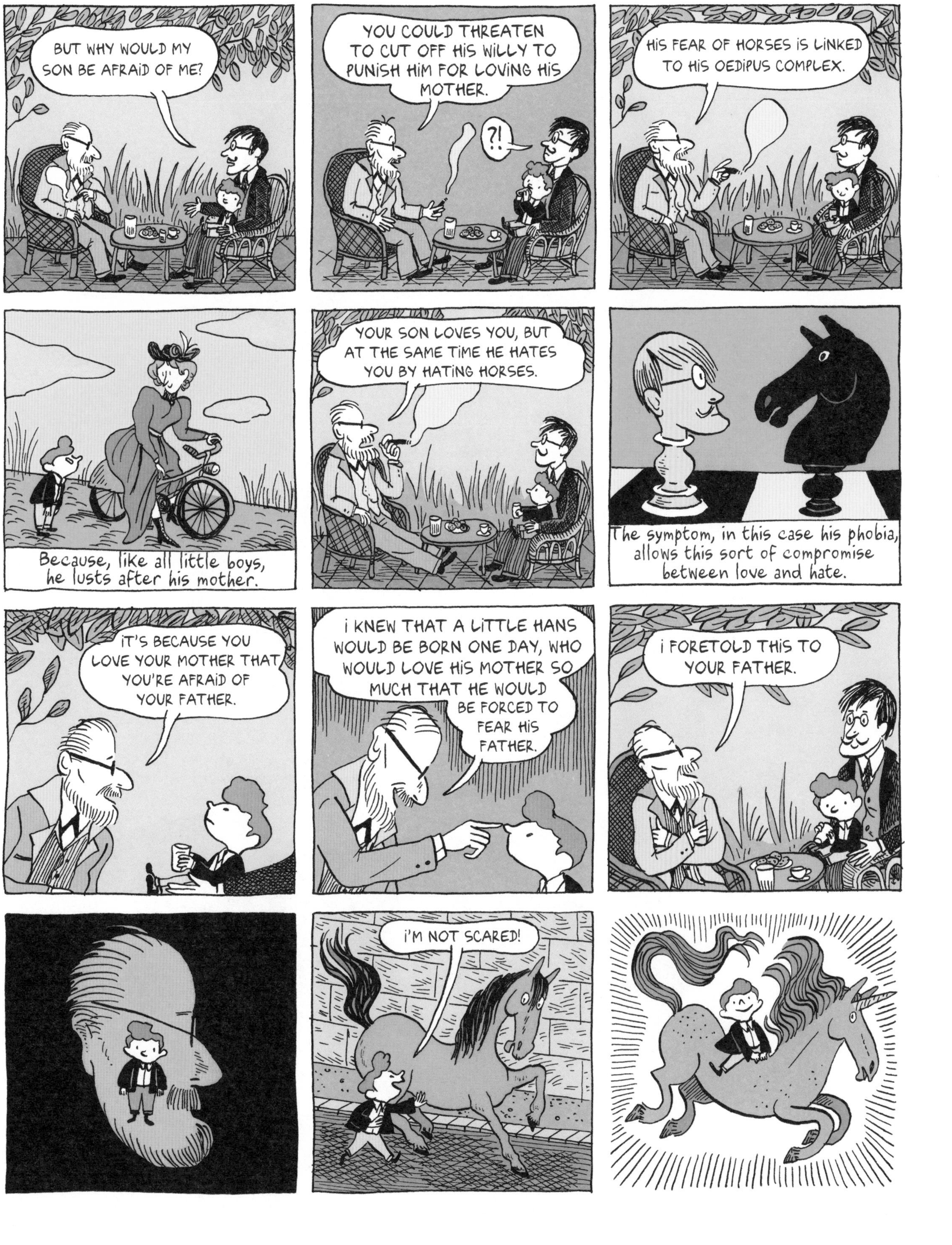
BUT WHY WOULD MY SON BE AFRAID OF ME?
YOU COULD THREATEN TO CUT OFF HIS WILLY TO PUNISH HIM FOR LOVING HIS MOTHER.
?!
HIS FEAR OF HORSES IS LINKED TO HIS OEDIPUS COMPLEX.
Because, like all little boys, he lusts after his mother.
YOUR SON LOVES YOU, BUT AT THE SAME TIME HE HATES YOU BY HATING HORSES.
The symptom, in this case his phobia, allows this sort of compromise between love and hate.
IT'S BECAUSE YOU LOVE YOUR MOTHER THAT YOU'RE AFRAID OF YOUR FATHER.
I KNEW THAT A LITTLE HANS WOULD BE BORN ONE DAY, WHO WOULD LOVE HIS MOTHER SO MUCH THAT HE WOULD BE FORCED TO FEAR HIS FATHER.
I FORETOLD THIS TO YOUR FATHER.
I'M NOT SCARED!

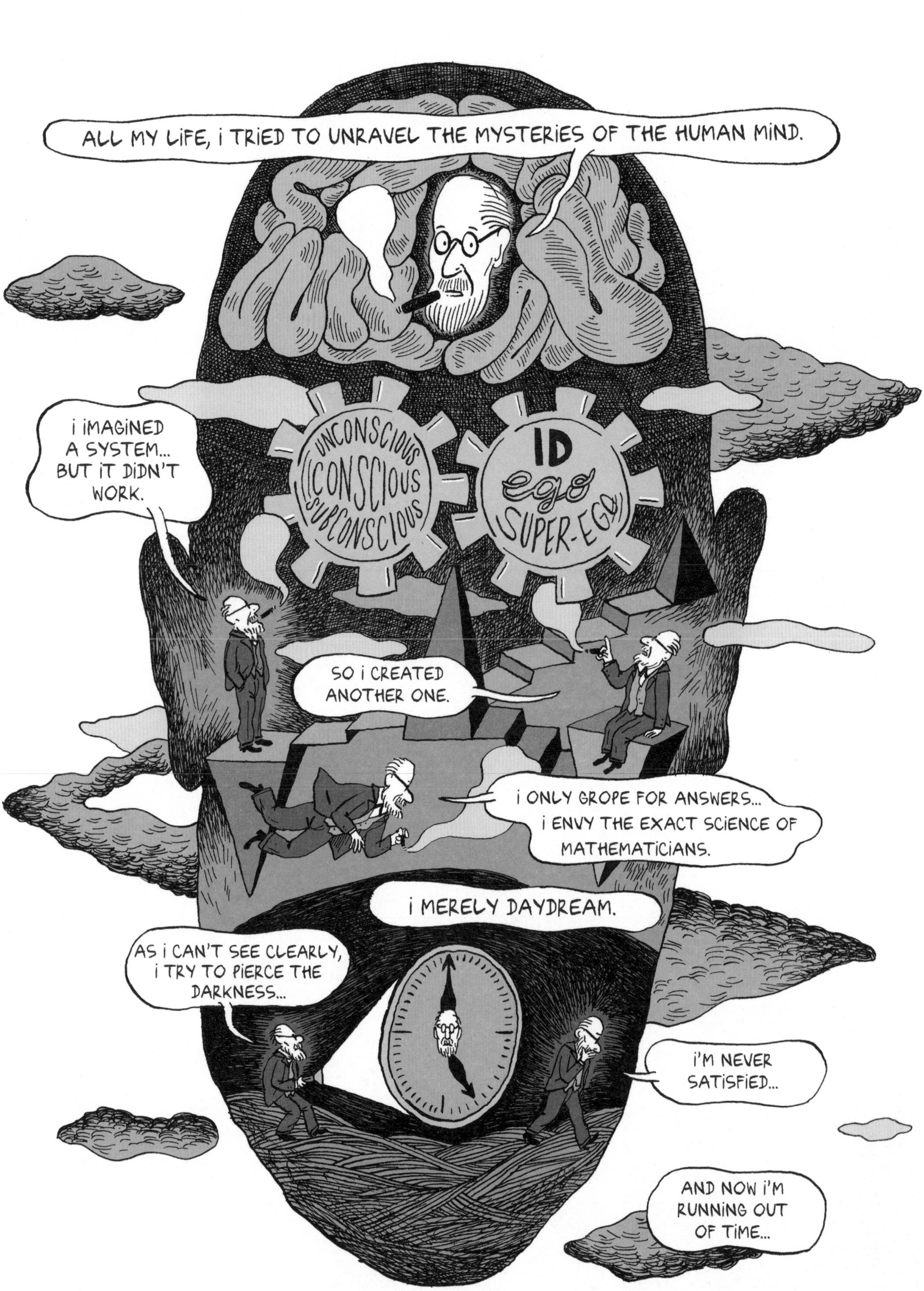
ALL MY LIFE, I TRIED TO UNRAVEL THE MYSTERIES OF THE HUMAN MIND.
I IMAGINED A SYSTEM... BUT IT DIDN'T WORK.
UNCONSCIOUS CONSCIOUS SUBCONSCIOUS
ID ego SUPER-EGO
SO I CREATED ANOTHER ONE.
I ONLY GROPE FOR ANSWERS... I ENVY THE EXACT SCIENCE OF MATHEMATICIANS.
I MERELY DAYDREAM.
AS I CAN'T SEE CLEARLY, I TRY TO PIERCE THE DARKNESS...
I'M NEVER SATISFIED...
AND NOW I'M RUNNING OUT OF TIME...

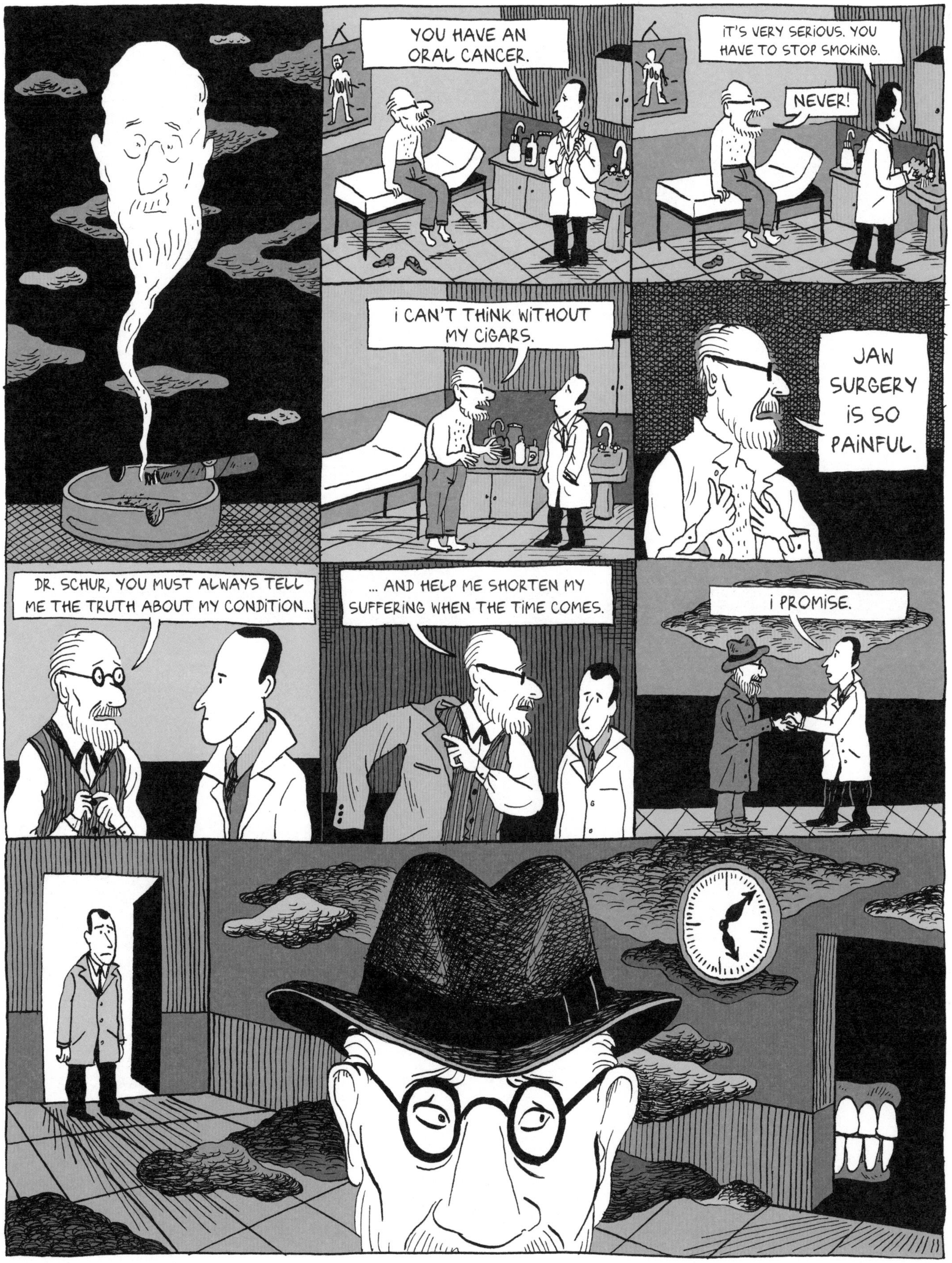
YOU HAVE AN ORAL CANCER.
IT'S VERY SERIOUS. YOU HAVE TO STOP SMOKING.
NEVER!
I CAN'T THINK WITHOUT MY CIGARS.
JAW SURGERY IS SO PAINFUL.
DR. SCHUR, YOU MUST ALWAYS TELL ME THE TRUTH ABOUT MY CONDITION...
... AND HELP ME SHORTEN MY SUFFERING WHEN THE TIME COMES.
I PROMISE.

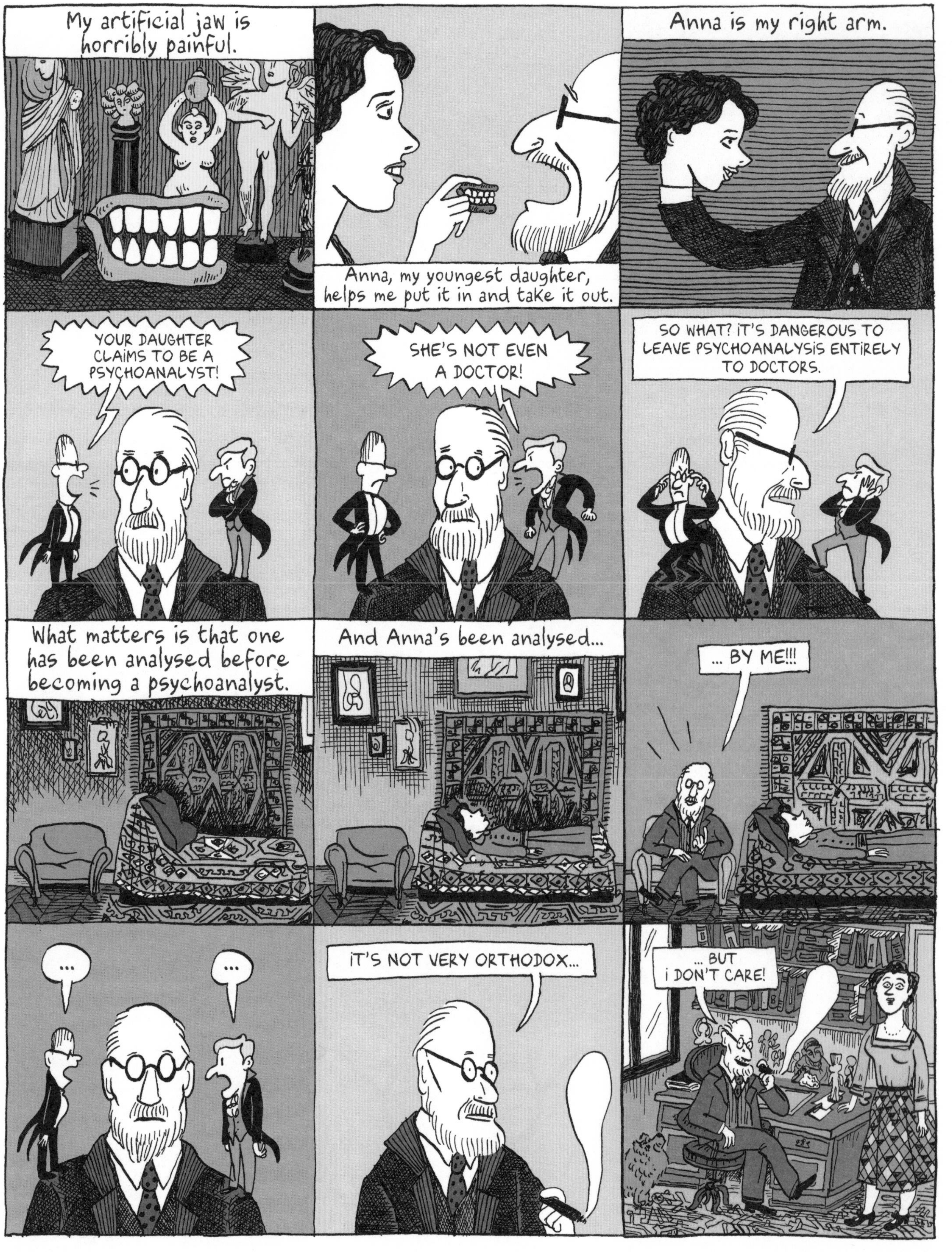

My artificial jaw is horribly painful.
Anna, my youngest daughter, helps me put it in and take it out.
Anna is my right arm.
YOUR DAUGHTER CLAIMS TO BE A PSYCHOANALYST!
SHE'S NOT EVEN A DOCTOR!
SO WHAT? IT'S DANGEROUS TO LEAVE PSYCHOANALYSIS ENTIRELY TO DOCTORS.
What matters is that one has been analysed before becoming a psychoanalyst.
And Anna's been analysed...
... BY ME!!!
...
...
IT'S NOT VERY ORTHODOX...
... BUT I DON'T CARE!

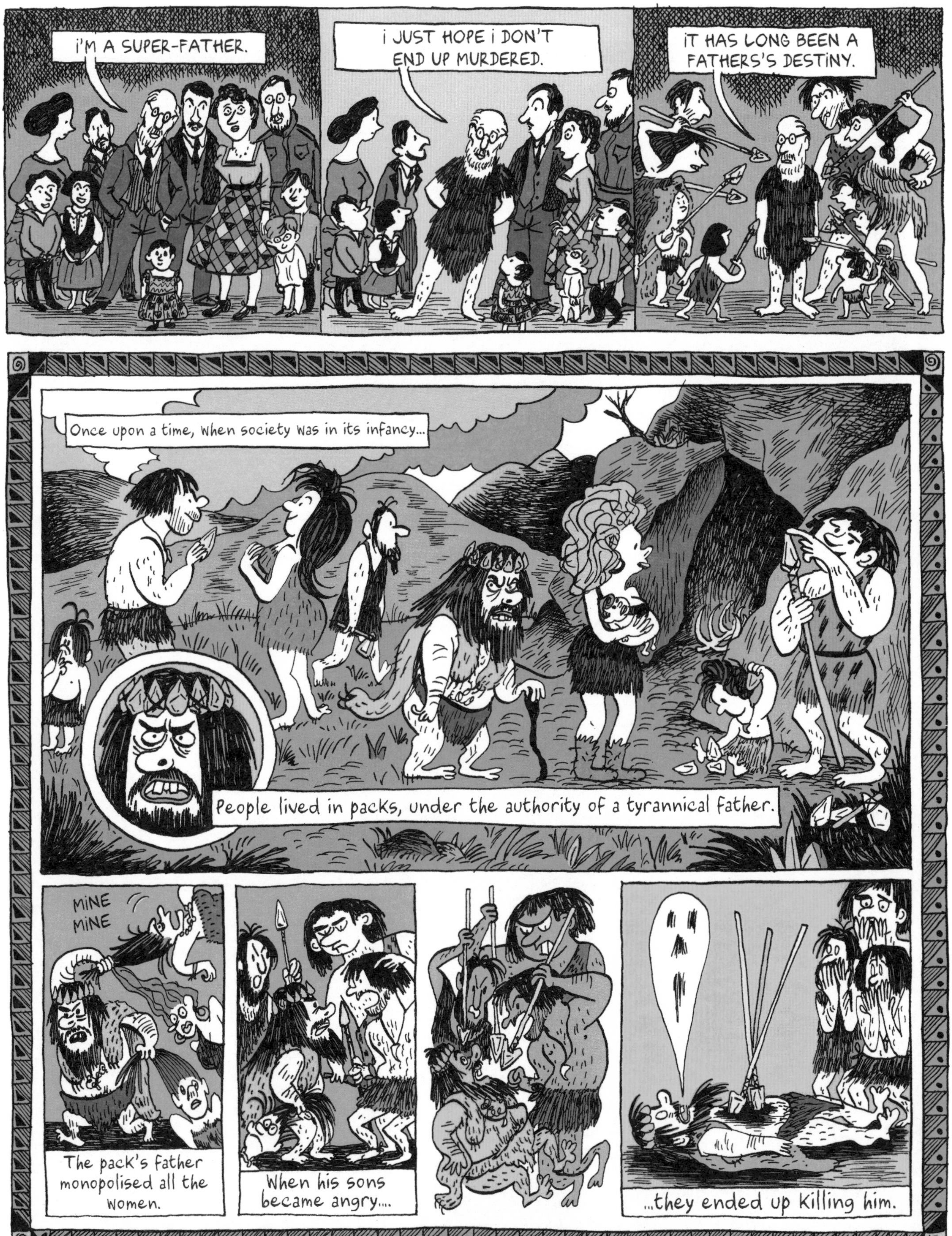

i'M A SUPER-FATHER.
i JUST HOPE i DON'T END UP MURDERED.
iT HAS LONG BEEN A FATHERS'S DESTiNY.
Once upon a time, when society was in its infancy...
People lived in packs, under the authority of a tyrannical father.
MiNE MiNE
The pack's father monopolised all the women.
When his sons became angry....
...they ended up killing him.

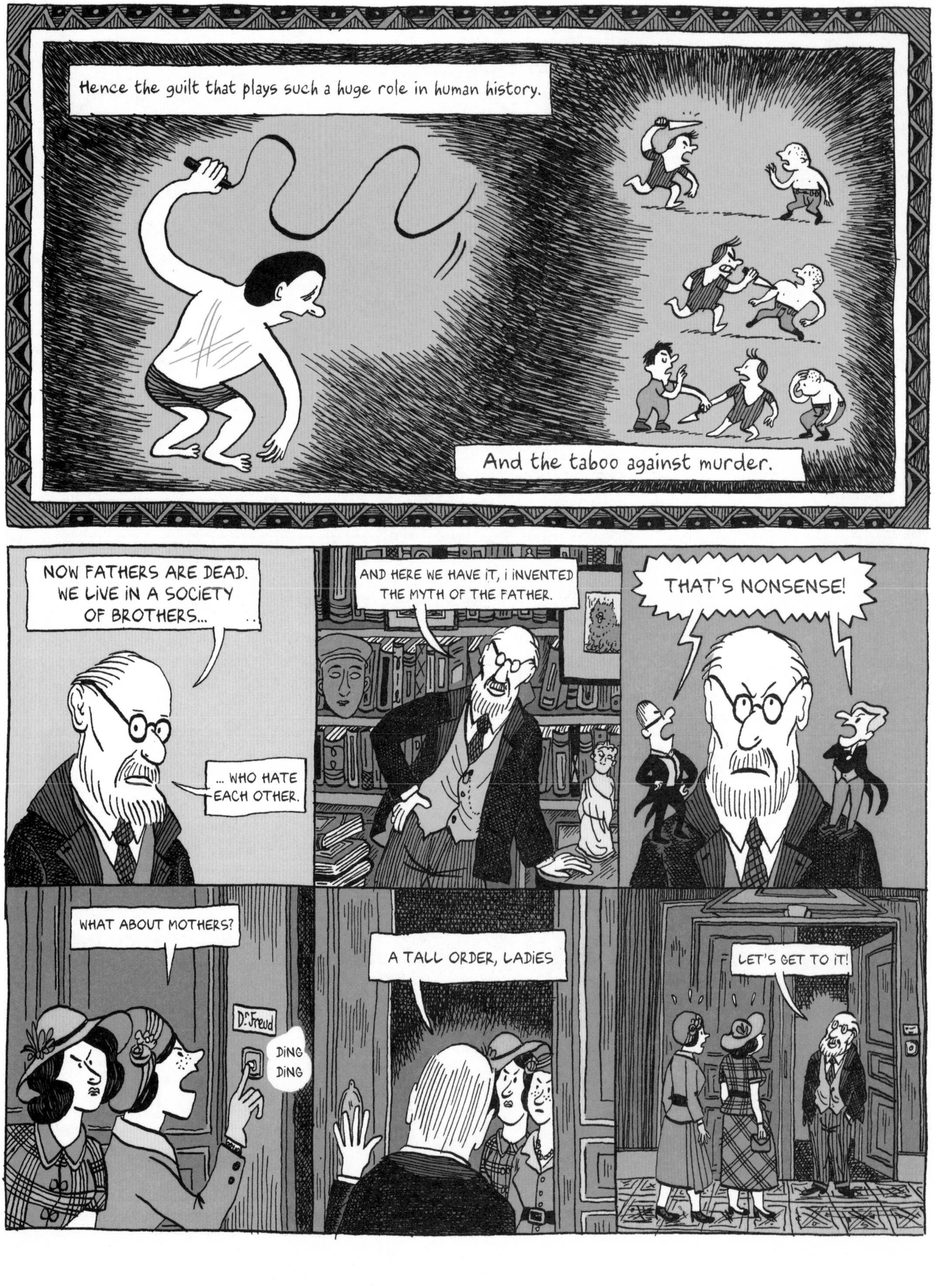
Hence the guilt that plays such a huge role in human history.
And the taboo against murder.
NOW FATHERS ARE DEAD. WE LIVE IN A SOCIETY OF BROTHERS...
... WHO HATE EACH OTHER.
AND HERE WE HAVE IT, I INVENTED THE MYTH OF THE FATHER.
THAT'S NONSENSE!
WHAT ABOUT MOTHERS?
Dr Freud
DING DING
A TALL ORDER, LADIES
LET'S GET TO IT!

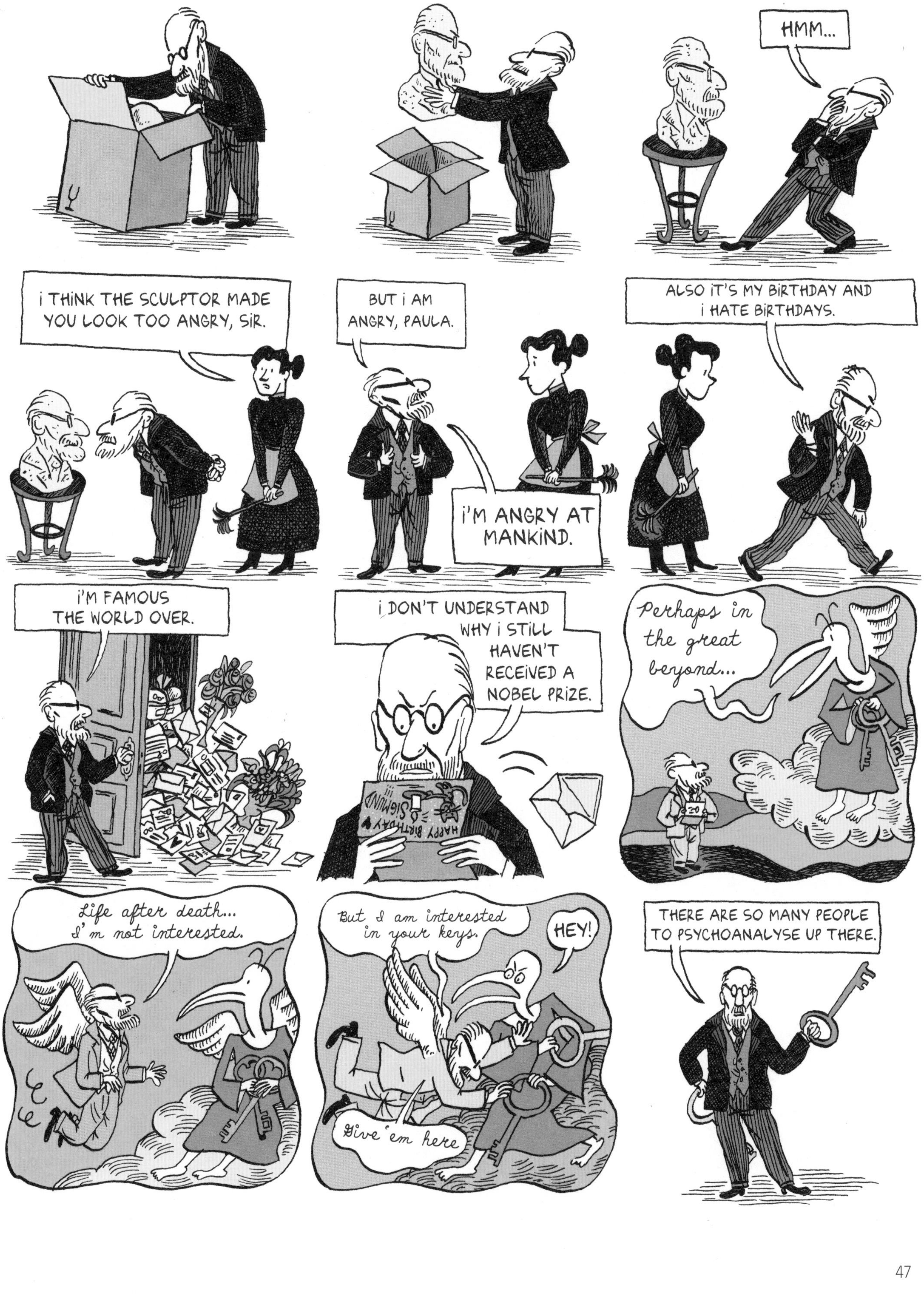
HMM...
i THINK THE SCULPTOR MADE YOU LOOK TOO ANGRY, SiR.
BUT i AM ANGRY, PAULA.
i'M ANGRY AT MANKiND.
ALSO iT'S MY BiRTHDAY AND i HATE BiRTHDAYS.
i'M FAMOUS THE WORLD OVER.
i DON'T UNDERSTAND WHY i STiLL HAVEN'T RECEiVED A NOBEL PRiZE.
HAPPY BIRTHDAY SIGMUND!!!
Perhaps in the great beyond...
Life after death... I'm not interested.
But I am interested in your keys.
HEY!
Give 'em here
THERE ARE SO MANY PEOPLE TO PSYCHOANALYSE UP THERE.

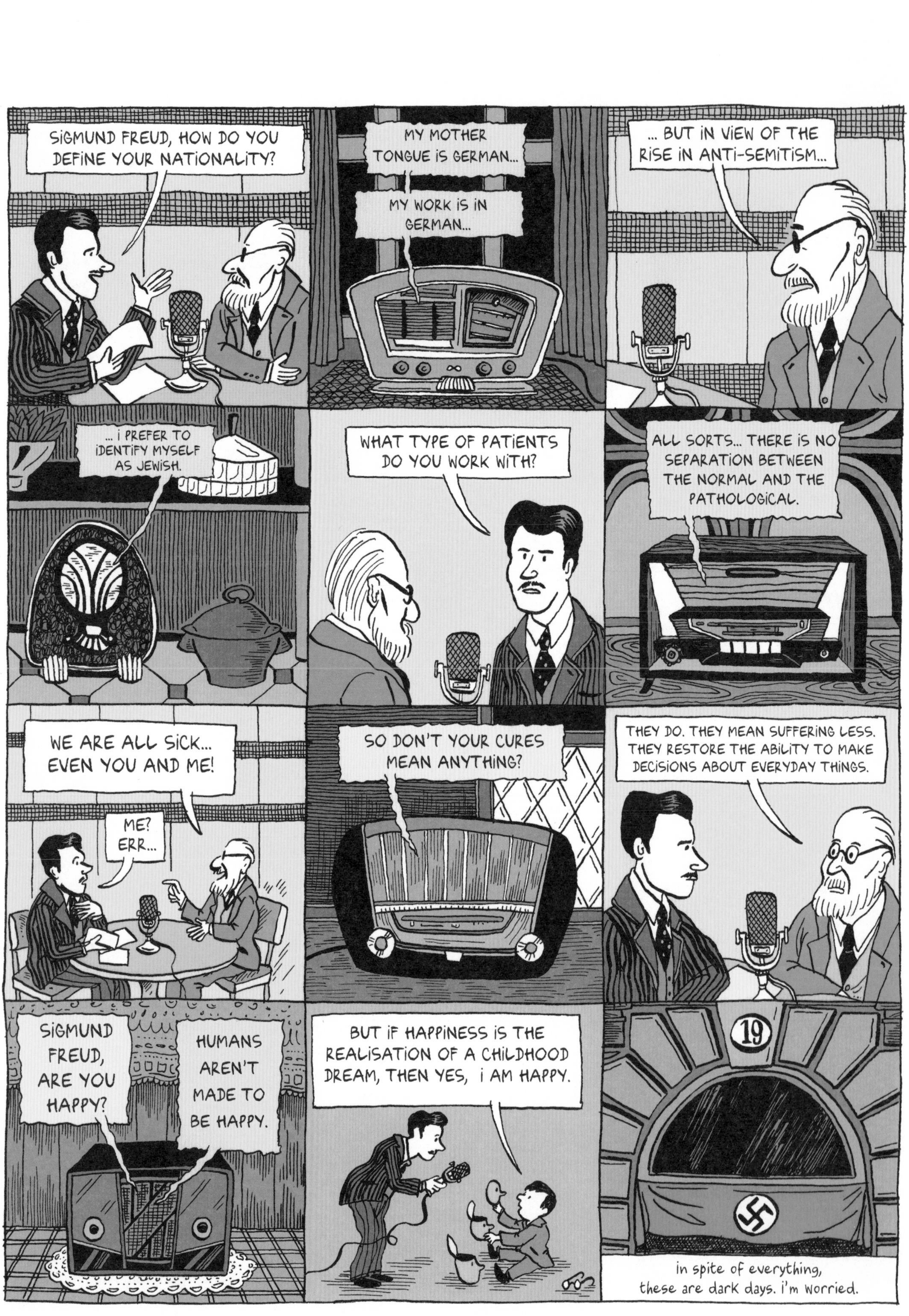
SIGMUND FREUD, HOW DO YOU DEFINE YOUR NATIONALITY?
MY MOTHER TONGUE IS GERMAN...
MY WORK IS IN GERMAN...
... BUT IN VIEW OF THE RISE IN ANTI-SEMITISM...
... I PREFER TO IDENTIFY MYSELF AS JEWISH.
WHAT TYPE OF PATIENTS DO YOU WORK WITH?
ALL SORTS... THERE IS NO SEPARATION BETWEEN THE NORMAL AND THE PATHOLOGICAL.
WE ARE ALL SICK... EVEN YOU AND ME!
ME? ERR...
SO DON'T YOUR CURES MEAN ANYTHING?
THEY DO. THEY MEAN SUFFERING LESS. THEY RESTORE THE ABILITY TO MAKE DECISIONS ABOUT EVERYDAY THINGS.
SIGMUND FREUD, ARE YOU HAPPY?
HUMANS AREN'T MADE TO BE HAPPY.
BUT IF HAPPINESS IS THE REALISATION OF A CHILDHOOD DREAM, THEN YES, I AM HAPPY.
19
in spite of everything, these are dark days. i'm worried.

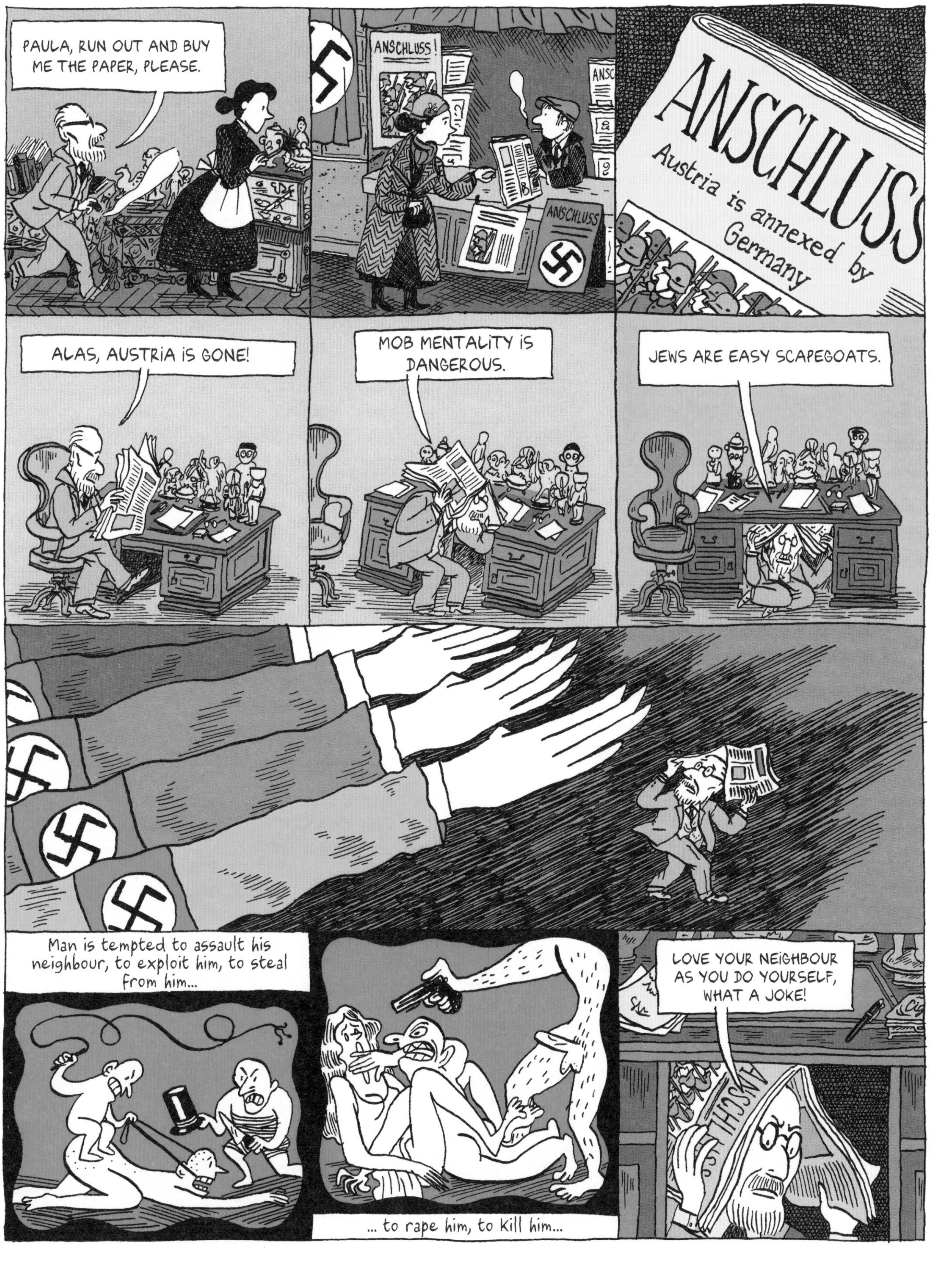
PAULA, RUN OUT AND BUY ME THE PAPER, PLEASE.
ANSCHLUSS!
ANSCHLUSS
ANSCHLUSS
Austria is annexed by Germany
ALAS, AUSTRIA IS GONE!
MOB MENTALITY IS DANGEROUS.
JEWS ARE EASY SCAPEGOATS.
Man is tempted to assault his neighbour, to exploit him, to steal from him...
... to rape him, to kill him...
LOVE YOUR NEIGHBOUR AS YOU DO YOURSELF, WHAT A JOKE!

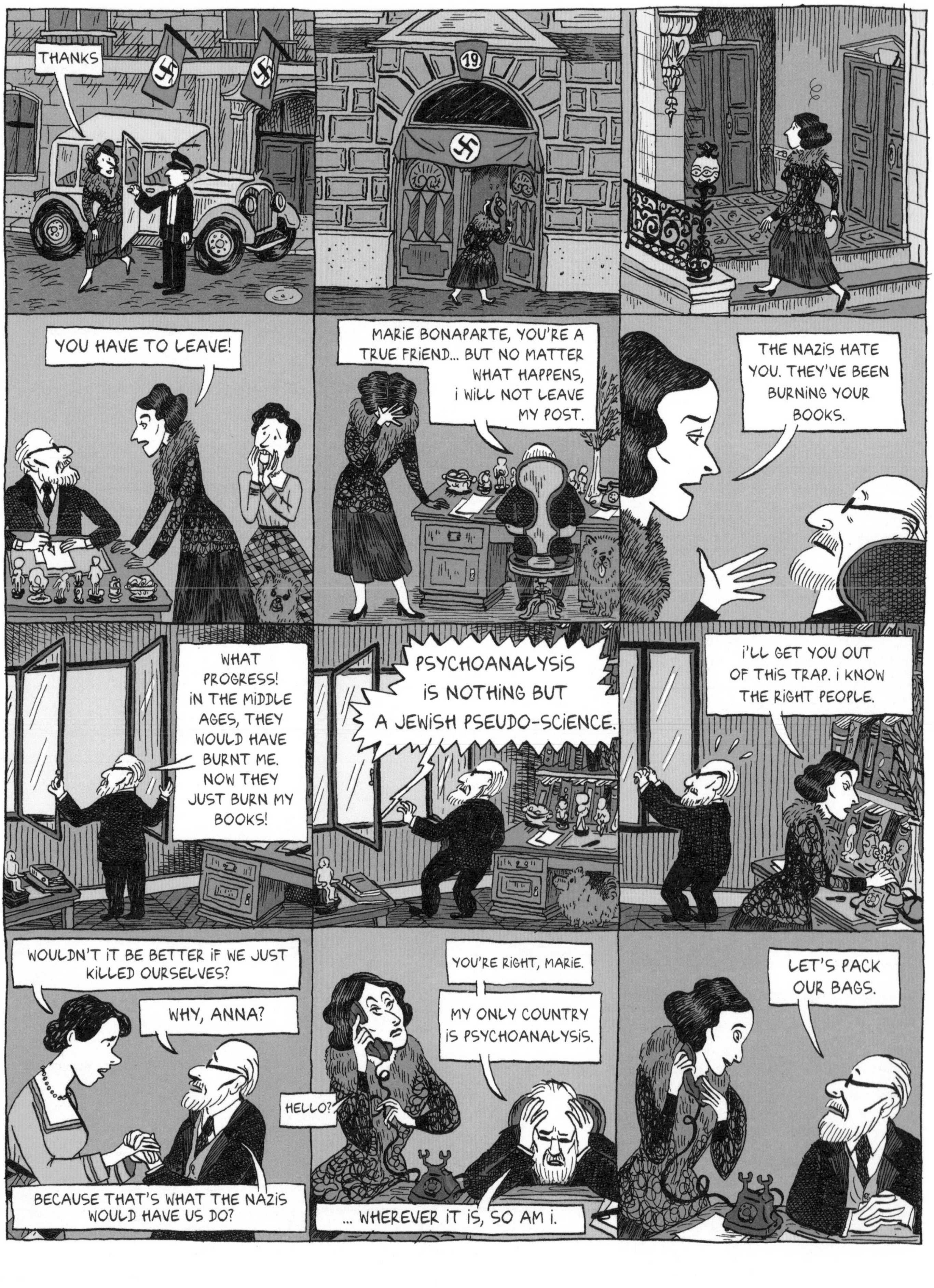
THANKS
19
YOU HAVE TO LEAVE!
MARIE BONAPARTE, YOU'RE A TRUE FRIEND... BUT NO MATTER WHAT HAPPENS, I WILL NOT LEAVE MY POST.
THE NAZIS HATE YOU. THEY'VE BEEN BURNING YOUR BOOKS.
WHAT PROGRESS! IN THE MIDDLE AGES, THEY WOULD HAVE BURNT ME. NOW THEY JUST BURN MY BOOKS!
PSYCHOANALYSIS IS NOTHING BUT A JEWISH PSEUDO-SCIENCE.
I'LL GET YOU OUT OF THIS TRAP. I KNOW THE RIGHT PEOPLE.
WOULDN'T IT BE BETTER IF WE JUST KILLED OURSELVES?
WHY, ANNA?
BECAUSE THAT'S WHAT THE NAZIS WOULD HAVE US DO?
HELLO?
YOU'RE RIGHT, MARIE.
MY ONLY COUNTRY IS PSYCHOANALYSIS.
... WHEREVER IT IS, SO AM I.
LET'S PACK OUR BAGS.

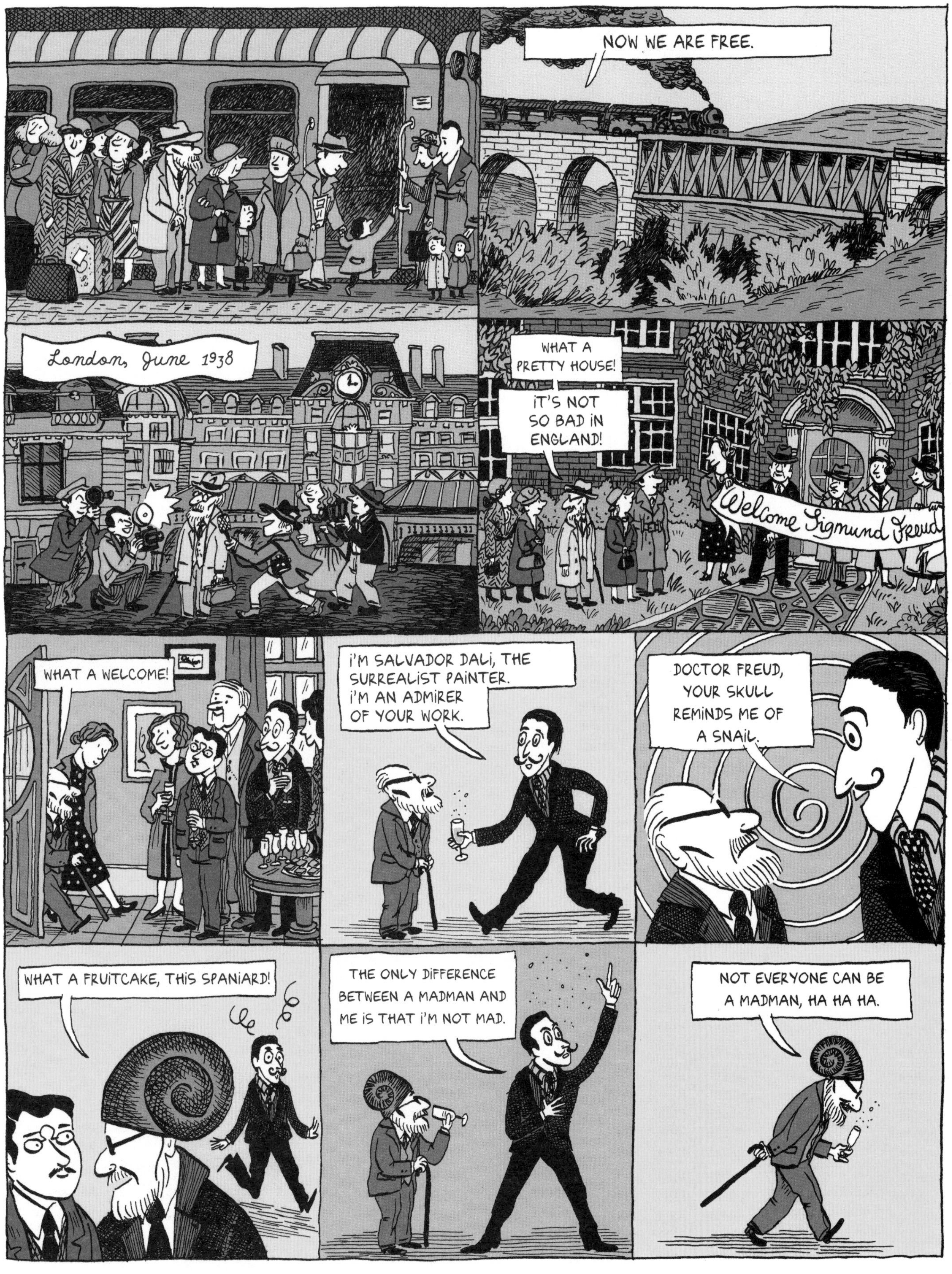
NOW WE ARE FREE.
London, June 1938
WHAT A PRETTY HOUSE!
IT'S NOT SO BAD IN ENGLAND!
Welcome Sigmund Freud
WHAT A WELCOME!
I'M SALVADOR DALI, THE SURREALIST PAINTER. I'M AN ADMIRER OF YOUR WORK.
DOCTOR FREUD, YOUR SKULL REMINDS ME OF A SNAIL.
WHAT A FRUITCAKE, THIS SPANIARD!
THE ONLY DIFFERENCE BETWEEN A MADMAN AND ME IS THAT I'M NOT MAD.
NOT EVERYONE CAN BE A MADMAN, HA HA HA.

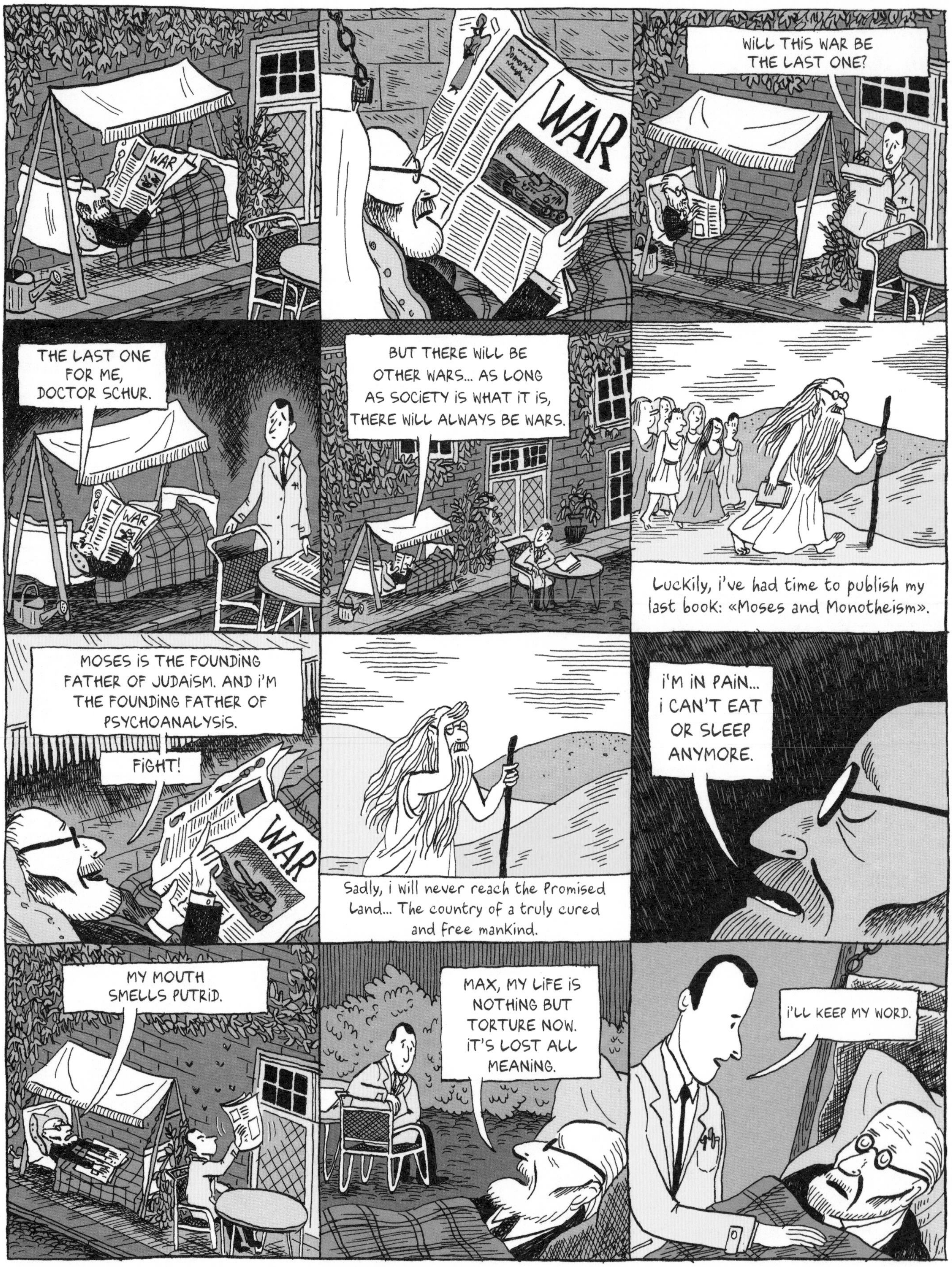
WAR
WAR
WiLL THIS WAR BE THE LAST ONE?
THE LAST ONE FOR ME, DOCTOR SCHUR.
WAR
BUT THERE WiLL BE OTHER WARS... AS LONG AS SOCiETY iS WHAT iT iS, THERE WiLL ALWAYS BE WARS.
Luckily, i've had time to publish my last book: «Moses and Monotheism».
MOSES iS THE FOUNDiNG FATHER OF JUDAiSM. AND i'M THE FOUNDiNG FATHER OF PSYCHOANALYSiS.
FiGHT!
WAR
Sadly, i will never reach the Promised Land... The country of a truly cured and free mankind.
i'M iN PAiN... i CAN'T EAT OR SLEEP ANYMORE.
MY MOUTH SMELLS PUTRiD.
MAX, MY LiFE iS NOTHiNG BUT TORTURE NOW. iT'S LOST ALL MEANiNG.
i'LL KEEP MY WORD.

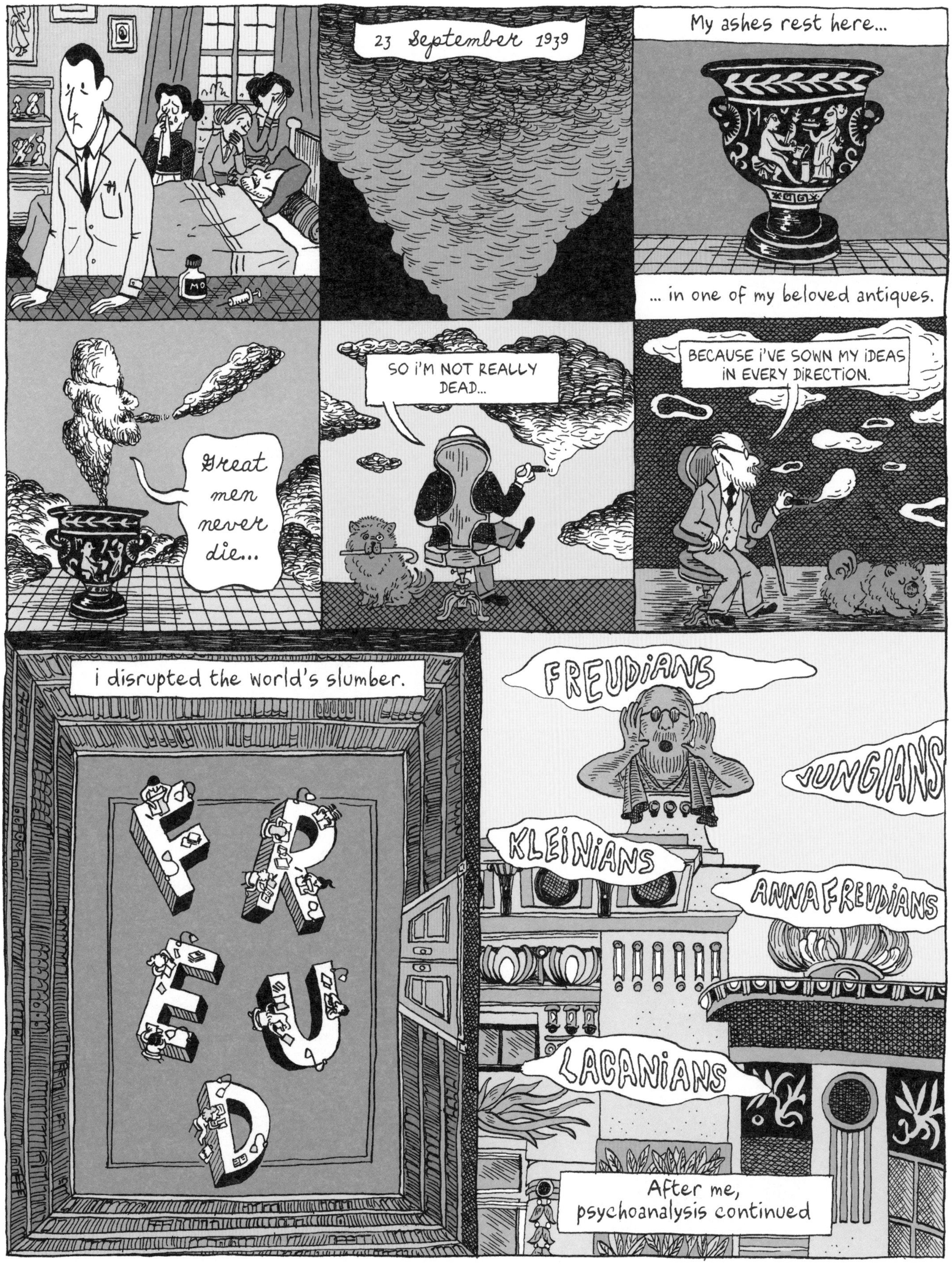
23 September 1939
My ashes rest here...
... in one of my beloved antiques.
Great men never die...
SO I'M NOT REALLY DEAD...
BECAUSE I'VE SOWN MY IDEAS IN EVERY DIRECTION.
I disrupted the world's slumber.
FREUD
FREUDIANS
JUNGIANS
KLEINIANS
ANNAFREUDIANS
LACANIANS
After me, psychoanalysis continued

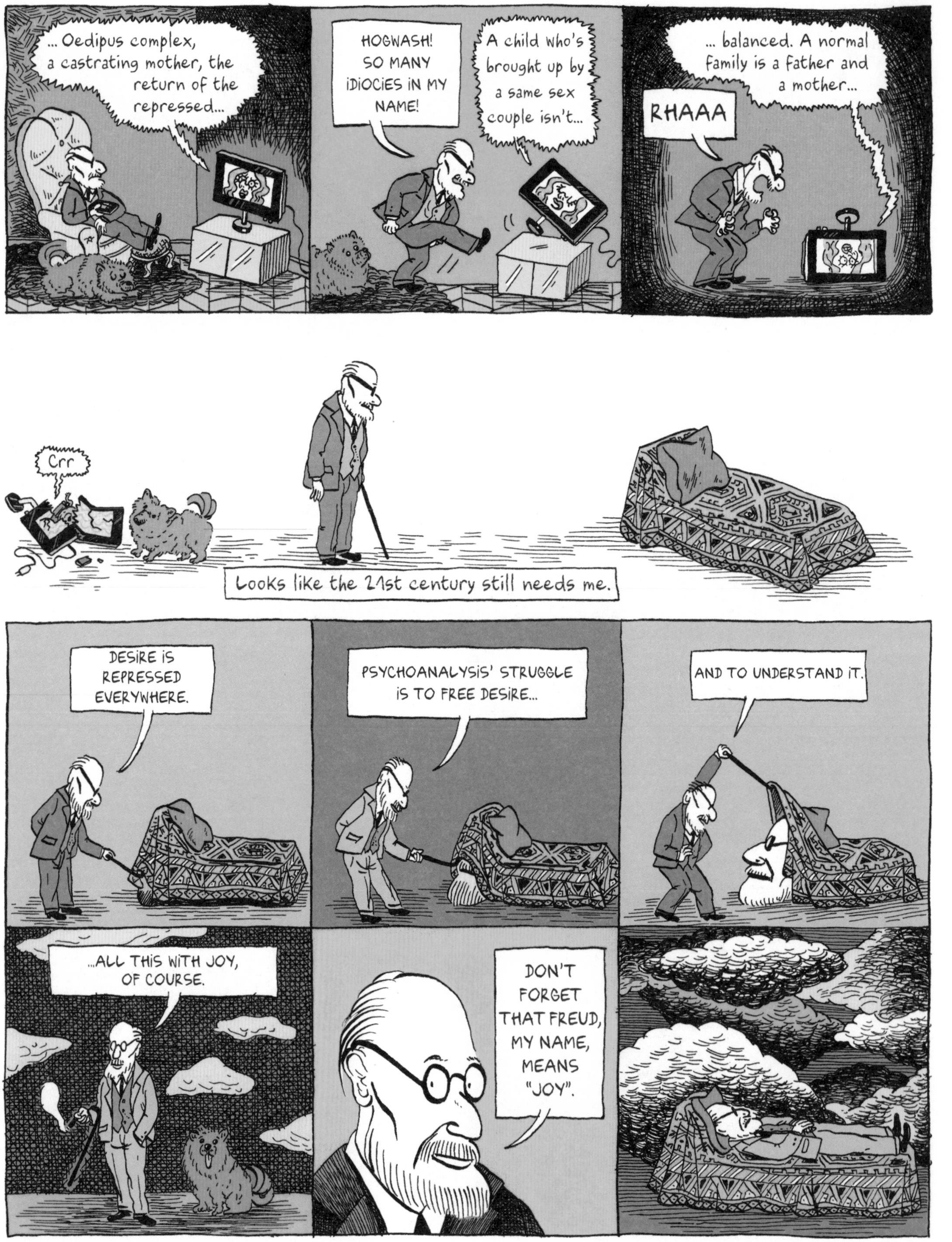

... Oedipus complex, a castrating mother, the return of the repressed...
HOGWASH! SO MANY IDIOCIES IN MY NAME!
A child who's brought up by a same sex couple isn't...
... balanced. A normal family is a father and a mother...
RHAAA
Crr
Looks like the 21st century still needs me.
DESIRE IS REPRESSED EVERYWHERE.
PSYCHOANALYSIS' STRUGGLE IS TO FREE DESIRE...
AND TO UNDERSTAND IT.
...ALL THIS WITH JOY, OF COURSE.
DON'T FORGET THAT FREUD, MY NAME, MEANS "JOY".

Auf wiedersehen!

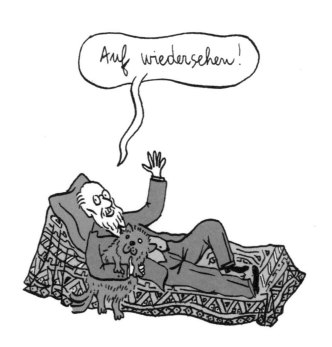

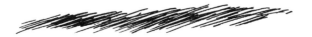

ALSO BY CORINNE MAIER AND ANNE SIMON

MARX, AN ILLUSTRATED BIOGRAPHY

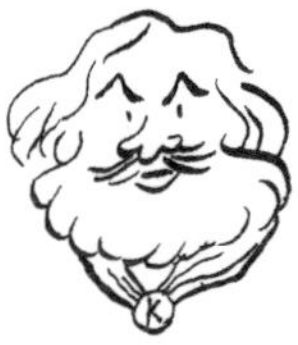

SELECTED BIBLIOGRAPHY

The interpretation of Dreams (1900)

The Psychopathology of Everyday Life (1901)

Jokes and their Relation to the Unconscious (1905)

Fragments of an Analysis of a Case of Hysteria (1905)

Analysis of a Phobia in a Five-year-old Boy (1909)

Notes Upon A Case of Obsessional Neurosis (1909)

Five Lectures on Psychoanalysis (1910)

Totem and Taboo (1912–1913)

Mourning and Melancholia (1917)

The Uncanny (1919)

Group Psychology And The Analysis Of The Ego (1921)

Neurosis and Psychosis (1924)

An Autobiographical Study (1925)

The Future of an illusion (1927)

Civilisation and its Discontents (1930)

Why War? (1933)

Moses and Monotheism (1939)